Archibald Campbell Tait

The present Condition Of The Church Of England

Archibald Campbell Tait

The present Condition Of The Church Of England

ISBN/EAN: 9783743349278

Manufactured in Europe, USA, Canada, Australia, Japa

Cover: Foto ©Lupo / pixelio.de

Manufactured and distributed by brebook publishing software (www.brebook.com)

Archibald Campbell Tait

The present Condition Of The Church Of England

OF THE

CHURCH OF ENGLAND.

SEVEN ADDRESSES

DELIVERED TO

THE CLERGY AND CHURCHWARDENS OF HIS DIOCESE,

AS

HIS CHARGE,

At his Primary Visitation,

1872.

BY

ARCHIBALD CAMPBELL,

ARCHBISHOP OF CANTERBURY.

London:
MACMILLAN AND CO.
1872.

[The Right of Translation and Reproduction is reserved.]

CONTENTS.

ADDRESSES.

	PAGE
I. Lay Co-operation	1
II. Cathedral Reform	14
III. Ecclesiastical Judicature	24
IV. Ecclesiastical Judicature (*continued*)	43
V. Ecclesiastical Legislation	55
VI. Missionary Work of the Church	71
VII. The Church of England in its relation to the rest of Christendom	86

APPENDICES.

A. Canterbury Diocesan Education Society	103
B. Canterbury Diocesan Church Building and Endowment Society	105
C. Note on the Statutes of Canterbury Cathedral	106
D. The Act of Uniformity Amendment Act, 1872	107
E. Society for the Relief of Widows and Orphans	114
F. Association of Lay Helpers	114
G. Confirmations in the Diocese	118
H. The Church Penitentiary Association, and the Stone Penitentiary	118
I. St. Peter's Orphan Home	120
K. Church of England Temperance Association	120
L. Special Services for 20th December	122

THE PRESENT CONDITION

OF

THE CHURCH OF ENGLAND.

ADDRESSES

ON THE

Present Position of the Church of England.

I.

(Delivered at Maidstone to the Deanery of Sutton, Tuesday, September 24.)

My Reverend Brethren, and my Brethren the Churchwardens:

I rejoice to have an opportunity of meeting you here. I have indeed, during the first year of my occupancy of this See, twice been amongst you already, but it pleased God to lay me aside, and at one time I scarcely expected that I should ever have the opportunity of meeting you as on this day. It is now four years since my revered predecessor announced his intention of holding a visitation. You are aware that death intervened. His last moments, I may almost say, were occupied with thoughts of his diocese; and when the unfinished Charge was published, which he was in the act of preparing when God removed him, no one could fail to be struck with that touching record of his last thoughts. His memory will ever live fresh in this diocese, and throughout the Church of England. Those who knew him personally saw that he was indeed a Christian in the highest sense of the word, and that the kindness which he exercised towards all flowed from the deepest Christian principle. Those who watched his career elsewhere know what he did for the Church of England on the first establishment of the diocese of Ripon in one of our great manufacturing districts; those who have followed his career at Durham and at York—though he remained there so short a time—know that his work in those dioceses was great; and through the six years during which he occupied this archiepiscopal chair, with indefatigable zeal—zeal beyond his health and years—he laboured for this diocese, and for the well-being of the whole Church. He held one visitation amongst you, but died while preparing for the second. He had made his usual visitation inquiries, and had arranged for the publication of the results as part of his Charge. And now the fourth year, the regular year of visitation, has returned. I trust that the Church has suffered no injury in the interval. In the first year of my Archiepiscopate I did indeed informally visit several deaneries throughout the diocese, and since that time the Archdeacon, the Bishop Suffragan, and the Rural Deans have, I doubt not, supplied what was lacking on my part. Now however, thank God, I am able to see you once again personally. I do not intend on this occasion to give in each place which I visit a lengthened Charge, for it seems to me that there is something unnatural in repeating, over and over again, the same words on the same subjects at the various centres of the visitation; and I therefore propose at each place to confine myself to an address on some one subject, and afterwards, if it please God, when the whole visitation is concluded, to publish the several Charges, so that they may form one document. Probably by this means I shall be better able to overtake the many subjects which press upon us at this time.

I will speak to-day on a matter greatly concerning the relative duties of the Clergy and Laity of the Church of England at this particular time. I am addressing many churchwardens, as well as clergy. The clergy and the churchwardens are intimately united in the work of our several parishes. The Church of England, according to its constitution, assigns an important part to the laity in the work of every parish; and I know, from my experience of the clergy both here and in the diocese of London, that I am only speaking their sentiments when I say that without the help of the laity they feel themselves powerless in the work that is committed to them. The very name of our office—"Ministers"—implies that we are the servants of God and His flock. And if we claim the name of "Presbyters," this is not as lords over God's heritage, but because we are appointed to stand forth, as might the head of a family, to direct, and guide, and help those who are committed to our care. The name of "Deacon" also, which marks another office in our ministry, implies that they who bear it are the servants at once of those who are set over them in the Lord, of Christ, and of His people. It is not a mere assumed and empty name if we call ourselves the servants of the servants of Christ; and we desire in all things to work for the good of the flock, that is, for the laity whom Christ has committed to us. And as in every society one member cannot prosper unless assisted by the others, so (I speak the feeling of the clergy when I say this) without the help of the laity we shall be powerless in the discharge of our great duties. Now, various plans have been suggested in the present day whereby the clergy and laity may work more heartily and more regularly together. We have heard of proposals made in the Legislature for establishing parochial councils, whereby the clergyman is to be called upon to confer with the laity, or some select body of the laity, on all difficult matters which concern his parish. We have heard also, and know by experience, the plans which have been much canvassed of late for holding large meetings of the clergy and laity. Such meetings, I believe, are held regularly in many of the rural deaneries of this diocese; and one meeting on a larger scale took place last autumn in the adjoining Archdeaconry of Canterbury. Such schemes cannot as yet any of them be supposed to have come to maturity. The scheme for Parochial Councils may or may not prove to be really for the good of the Church. Everything certainly which creates sympathy between clergy and laity is to be prized, and even if nothing else were gained by such schemes beyond the enlargement of a mutual sympathy amongst us, so far good would result. At the same time, with regard to all schemes of this kind, there seem to be two warnings which it is well to give.

None of these meetings or consultations will ever have any lasting effect if they are arranged upon any exclusive principle. We belong to a Church which glories in the name of National; and if it should turn out that any of our meetings were to assume a merely exclusive or party character, I think we should be acting against the spirit of the National Church. Men without regard to party, who are entitled by the constitution of the country and by the constitution of the Church to bear their part in Church matters, whosoever they be, ought to have an opportunity of joining in all such meetings.

The second warning which I would give is the very obvious one, that, if such meetings are to be of any use, they must be practical. Mere debating societies of the clergy and laity, loosely talking over the various questions which agitate the public mind, would, I think, very soon cease to have much interest for busy men in this busy age, and do upon the whole very little good. I am not speaking in disparagement of clerical societies or other societies which acknowledge that they have nothing for their object but the discussion of theological or ecclesiastical questions. But if the meetings of which I speak are to have any lasting influence upon the Church, they must have a distinctly practical character. Hence in the diocese of London, where we had some meetings of this kind, we endeavoured to connect them all with the distinctive work of the various societies which were labouring to extend the usefulness of the Church; and when I was invited last autumn to give some suggestions with reference to the great meeting of clergy and laity which took place in the adjoining Archdeaconry, I submitted to them the very practical question whether or not they desired to petition the Houses of Convocation and Parliament against or in favour of certain Bills which were then pending, and on the subject of which men's minds were much interested. So long as we find for such meetings distinct practical work, so long, I think, they can do nothing but good. But when they cease to be practical, they will cease to create any wide interest, and, ceasing to create a wide interest, they will very likely fall into the hands merely of a clique.

After all, however, these modes of uniting the clergy and laity, as I have said, are at present merely tentative, and perhaps but little progress has yet been made in the good work which is sought to be accomplished by those who have suggested them. Still we cannot suppose that the constitution of the Church of England does not find distinct room for the working of the clergy and laity together. What is this office of churchwarden which many of you here present hold? Does it not bear testimony to the fact that from the very earliest ages of the Church of England it has been the spirit of her constitution that the laity of the parish shall be fully represented in the church work that is carried on amongst us? The churchwardens, as you know, are chosen, one to represent the incumbent of the parish, another to represent the parishioners assembled in vestry, and both of them, whomsoever they represent, are the officers of the diocesan. Here, then, we have in the very nature of this office a representation of the laity, and a lay representation of the clergy; and we have also a representation of the central authority, submitting, of course, in all things to the decision of the law which regulates the whole Church, and thereby preventing each parish from acting independently by itself. A better constitution, I think, it would be difficult to find; and what I desire at this time to press upon the laymen who are here present is, that their duties as churchwardens are most truly important. If there ever was a time when they were important, they are so now. There is in some respects more difficulty than there was formerly in obtaining persons to hold the office of churchwarden, because the secular advantages which the administration of the public property conferred have disappeared. It is therefore more requisite that we should press upon all who are likely to be called to this office how great is the duty of assisting the clergy, the bishops, and the Church at large in the proper conduct of the affairs of each parish. We are thrown more than we were formerly upon our own resources—in other words, we are thrown more than ever upon the loyalty of those who desire the welfare of the Church and of Christ's people, and we feel that we shall not look to them in vain to discharge those duties which belong to their office, though circumstances have made them much more difficult to perform, and less attractive. I trust, therefore, that the churchwardens of this diocese will answer freely to the call that is made upon them, and that no one will ever think of refusing the office, when he feels that it is a means of doing good for Christ's sake to Christ's people. That regulation which implies that every churchwarden shall be a communicant, gives a higher idea of the office of churchwarden than has been generally entertained in times past by many who have held it. It seems to say that the man who holds that office should be one whose conduct is an example in the parish in which he is an officer: I trust every year we shall find more and more that the responsibilities of this office are deeply felt by those who are called to fill it, and that when a man comes to be the representative of his parish or of the clergyman of his parish, and the officer of his bishop, he will feel that he is bound to give an example, in his daily life and by his regular attendance upon religious ordinances, to the whole parish.

There are many ways in which the clergy in a well-regulated parish often avail themselves of the assistance of the laity. Among these are the visitation of the poor, and the efforts made to bring the children to school. In all these matters every clergyman must necessarily call in the assistance of his laity; and those laymen who take office in the Church seem to me to be bound, by the office they have assumed, to assist not only in more secular matters, but also in such good spiritual works as may fairly be required of them.

Moreover, beyond the limits of parish duty, the laity will find many opportunities of assisting the clergy in the work of every diocese. Great changes have come over the Church of England of late, and in nothing more than in the matter of education. We know what has been done in that respect even within the last three years, how a change has begun which we are only now working out. It is a long time since our Diocesan Education Society was established. Those who remember the state of things before the establishment of that Society can testify to the work—the importance of which it is almost impossible to measure—which has been done during those years. Now, of course, if the clergy had been left single-handed to establish that Diocesan Society, they would have been powerless. They appealed, and not in vain, to the laity; and schools have arisen amongst us in almost all places, and have been brought to their present state of excellence by the united action of the clergy and laity.[1] I am not forgetful of the fact, to which all acquainted with the subject bear testimony throughout the breadth of England, that the clergy with narrow means have exerted themselves far beyond their lay brethren for the extension of education, and that sums of money have been paid by them altogether out of proportion to what they receive for their services. But still, while they have freely given of their time and of their substance, they would be quite ready to testify, that, without the assistance of the laity, all their exertions and all their zeal would have failed. Now, this Diocesan Society appeals to you year after year for assistance, and there are many laymen who subscribe to it large and munificent sums; but I doubt whether it has as yet forced its way in all quarters on the notice of those who are bound to assist it, and whether there are not many laymen of ample means who fail to contribute to its funds, and so to help on that great work—perhaps the greatest committed to us—of educating the children of Christ's flock in the knowledge and love of God. I trust that this Society will receive more support in future than it has hitherto received from farmers, from tradesmen, and men of comparatively moderate means, and not only from the gentry who have large sums at their command.

I may remind you that it is no longer an open question whether or not there shall be a school in every neighbourhood. There must be a school; and parents will very soon find that their children are all obliged to attend. Let us, then, all exert ourselves to see that the training they receive in those schools is such as, being

[1] See Appendix A.

faithful to our Lord and Master, we can heartily approve. Now, I am told that in this particular town there is a very good supply of schools; that the effect of the recent legislation has been in no way to interfere with the religious character of those schools; and that the only result here has been the extremely good one, that a vast number of children who formerly did not receive any education have been gathered into the schools already existing at Maidstone. We must consider this to be a very happy result of recent legislation.

I do not expect that we are to have School Boards all over the country. It does not seem to me that that is a thing to be desired, or to be expected. School Boards are more or less expensive, and the ordinary expenses which fall upon ratepayers throughout the country are considerable already, and we do not particularly desire that they should be increased; but the only way to prevent this—if we wish to prevent it—must be by exerting ourselves to see that all children requiring education in our neighbourhood receive it, and that there are good schools to which they may be sent. I must therefore very strongly advise, as one mode in which the clergy and laity may co-operate in every parish, that the clergyman should put himself in communication with such laymen as he thinks will assist him in this matter, and that they should institute an inquiry as to whether there are any children who do not go to school, and by that moral persuasion which is more effective than even the compulsion of the law, should induce parents who are negligent to send their children to school; and then I trust that the new system will produce nothing but good; that we shall have, as we have had before, schools in which religion is distinctly taught, and that we shall also secure the great advantage of having the children who before were neglected gathered into schools where their eternal as well as temporal interests will be cared for.

There has been a certain amount of dissatisfaction in some places as to the progress that has been made by Church schools, but I feel quite sure that this dissatisfaction has no real ground. The arrangements made by our Church schools are such that they press on the conscience of no one. And a free rivalry between different sets of schools seems to me to be the most likely way by which a thoroughly good system of education, tending to the highest as well as to the mere temporary interests of the children, will be fostered throughout the country.

I have spoken of one of the societies in which the clergy and the laity of our diocese may thus co-operate. I must not forget another, which comes to us with the special recommendation at this time of having been founded by my honoured predecessor,—I mean the Church Building and Endowment Society. A very practical object for which the clergy and laity may meet in the several rural deaneries is to consider if there is any deficiency in our Church accommodation, or in the state of our churches, and endeavour, where necessary, to provide a remedy. I should be glad if many meetings for this Church Building Diocesan Society could be held amongst us. Archbishop Longley exerted himself greatly at the commencement of his Archiepiscopate for this Society. He was the founder of it; and he wrote far and wide to beg that all would take an interest in the work which he had so much at heart. The result was a great effort at first, but, as with many great efforts, there has since been a danger of its languishing. No one can go, as I have been going during the last few days, from church to church in this neighbourhood without being struck with the great improvement which has taken place in the condition of the Houses of God. This I consider to be greatly owing to the Diocesan Society. There is much more of that seemly appearance which we desire to see in the House of God—much more accommodation for the poor. Now here is a ready way in which clergy and laity may most advantageously and practically co-operate. Let them advance the interests of this central society which calls forth additional funds in every neighbourhood when once work is begun; but without the assistance of which, in most of the neighbourhoods, the work could not be begun at all. I therefore commend the Diocesan Church Building Society,[1] along with the Diocesan Education Society, to the earnest attention of both the clergy and laity here assembled.

My friends, it is a great work that lies before us. The Church of England has lasted for a long time, and, please God, we have resolved, that with more or less of its present constitution, it shall last till the Lord comes —that it shall last at least till it has done the work for which Christ guided men's hearts to give it its present organization. Doubtless over the unknown future we have no control; but this at least we can do, each of us, while our own day lasts—we can labour heartily and faithfully for the Lord we serve, and preserve the great inheritance He has committed to our trust. Men talk as

[1] See Appendix B.

if the Church of England were exposed at this time to dangers such as it has never known before. No doubt many of its external supports have fallen away from it, but there is no external support to be compared with that loyalty of spirit—that earnest desire for men's souls —which the grace of God has stirred in men's hearts, far more than in the generations which are passed. If we live in a time of difficulty and trial, we also live in a time when we have many encouragements, and when a zeal for the cause we have at heart is certainly spread widely throughout the land. The Church of England has always boasted that it is a National Church, and I suppose that no one knows anything of the British nation without knowing that there must be in it, as it consists of a great body of freemen, very considerable diversities of opinion. I trust that the Church of England never will forget that in the widest of those diversities of opinion there may be that essential unity which has bound together Christians of a thousand lands from generation to generation in the love of their one Lord, though each, according to his own best ability, and according to his own views, may choose the mode by which he deems the kingdom of his Lord may best be advanced. If we differ, we still agree. We agree in the love of Christ, and in the full recognition of the glorious Gospel of Christ. Evil would be the day if any one of the parties in the Church of England were to expel the other. Each is able to help the other forward, and I think that the diversities of opinion of which some of us are apt to complain are as nothing compared with the essential unity which makes us live in the desire to serve Him Who has bought us with His own blood.

II.

(Delivered at Canterbury to the Cathedral Body, Wednesday, October 2.)

My Reverend Brethren, and my Brethren the Lay Members of this Cathedral body:

Let me first express, in the name of you all, our thankfulness to Almighty God that we are assembled again within this ancient building, and that the danger which threatened it a short time ago has passed away. It is indeed a great cause for thankfulness that this storehouse of religious and historical associations has been spared entire, and I am sure I am only expressing your feelings when I say how thankful we are to all those who by their exertions on that occasion contributed to the preservation of this noble pile.[1]

It has been customary in this Cathedral from time immemorial that there shall be every four years a visitation of the Cathedral body—a custom which is not generally observed in the other Cathedrals of England, but I think it is a wholesome and a good custom; it brings us face to face with one another, and enables us to review our several responsibilities,

---

[1] The fire which broke out in Canterbury Cathedral on the morning of September 3rd, was by the great exertions of the citizens and others suppressed without extending farther than the external roof of the Choir.

and, if anything is lacking, to apply ourselves at once to improvement.

I cannot meet you this day without recalling to memory in the first place that venerable man whose chair I now occupy. I have already elsewhere expressed my feelings as to the great services which in his generation he rendered to the Church of England. Still less, meeting you here to-day as the Cathedral body, can I forget the great loss which this Church sustained scarcely two years ago. When I speak of Dean Alford, I remember that he was my friend, and therefore as his friend I mourn his departure. But no feelings of mere personal regard need mingle on such an occasion with our regrets. Those who knew him in his public capacity, the crowds who heard him in London, the large numbers who came to this Cathedral to hear him speak from the pulpit, the vast number of persons throughout the whole of England to whom his ample stores of learning opened an access to knowledge which they could not otherwise have attained,—all attest his worth. The zeal with which he applied himself during the years when he was Dean of Canterbury to make this Cathedral in all respects what he desired it should be—a Church to the glory of God and the good of man; that peculiar position which he occupied—and which I may say almost he alone occupied—in the Church of England in reference to the great Nonconforming communities; —these things prevent us from forgetting this day the loss which the Church of England has sustained. The last point upon which I have touched is one upon which there may be diversity of opinion; but I, for my part, consider it a great blessing that we had amongst us a man whose conscientious convictions enabled him to mix with Christians of all kinds. True to the traditions of this place, which offered a sanctuary in time of danger to the persecuted Protestants of the Continent, he was enabled, from his longing after perfect communion with all who served his Lord, to unite with many from whom others are by conscientious convictions separated, and to make it understood that the faithful minister and leader of the Church of England has a heart as wide as the Church of Christ. Doubtless now he enjoys that full communion with the saints which his heart longed for during the years of his earthly ministrations.

But we who are met here to-day have more to do with the present and the future than we have with the past. Many of us are old enough to remember the great changes which have in this century come over the Church of England, and not least over our Cathedral institutions. None of us can tell what changes are in store for us in the time to come; but we can, and I trust do, all resolve, that whether our present system remain the same or be changed, we will fulfil the duties of the great position to which God Almighty has called us as members of this Cathedral Church. I would desire, therefore, that we should for a few moments set before our minds the ideal we entertain of a Cathedral body, and should endeavour to consider how far we are enabled to fulfil the duties which that ideal implies. I shall feel grateful to the Dean and Chapter if, when the formal business of this week is over, they will place in my hands the statutes and ordinances by which the Cathedral is administered,[1] that we may consider any suggestions

[1] See Appendix C.

made as to the best means of fulfilling the duties which those who founded the institution have laid upon us.

I suppose the first and greatest duty of Cathedral bodies is to afford means for the worship of Almighty God, that the worship may be celebrated with all the solemnity which the system of our Church supplies; and I think here in Canterbury we shall find great care is taken that our services be such as become Him whom we worship. Nevertheless, it may be well for us to consider that late events have pointed to the possibility of some amendment being made for the better regulation of the system of our Cathedral worship. I think it is impossible for anyone who has been in the habit of constantly attending our Cathedral not to have been at times struck with the thought that a little more is sacrificed to the exquisite music with which our worship is adorned than perhaps is conducive to the real devotional spirit of the great majority of those who gather in our Church. I mean for example the daily substitution of what are technically called Services in lieu of simple chants.

An Act of Parliament passed last session distinctly recognized the fact that, wherever it was thought desirable, the order of our worship, whether in our Cathedrals or parochial churches, might be so modified as should be found most conducive to the edification of the worshippers. Far be it from me, with very limited experience of what is desirable in such places as this, to express an opinion whether you ought to avail yourselves of this option or no; but this I think is due to the Houses of Parliament which passed that Act, and to the Convocations by which it was recommended to the

Legislature, that you should carefully consider whether or no it suggests any improvement in your form of worship.

The next point which we ought to dwell on in our Cathedral establishments is, that as our buildings are great places for the service of Almighty God, for the singing of His praises, and for prayer, so also they are great places where vast congregations may be gathered together to hear the Word of God preached. Now, the experience of the last few years has shown that in an age which (to hear how men talk) you would often suppose was regardless of preaching, the influence of the pulpit remains as great as it ever was. Witness those vast congregations gathered together under the dome of St. Paul's, the revival of the wonderful preachings so familiar to all students of the Reformation at Paul's Cross. Witness the vast crowds gathered together in the great Abbey of Westminster. Witness similar assemblages in some of our country Cathedrals. Men are as ready now as they ever were to listen to the preaching of the Word of God when it is addressed to them with power, when the words and truths of the Gospel find an echo in their hearts from the voice of the preacher who speaks from heart to heart. Now, I venture to lay before this body the propriety of very carefully considering how far in this respect this or any other Cathedral comes up to the ideal which we ought to propose to ourselves. It is the system of the Church of Rome that it selects its preachers for no reason except that they are able to preach well. It seems desirable that, in a Cathedral where vast numbers may with the greatest propriety be assembled together, everything should be done to secure the best possible preaching which is to be found in the diocese or in the kingdom. Doubting not that the present arrangements are conducive to this object, I still think it may be well for us to consider whether in this respect we may not improve upon the progress we have already made. By the constitution of this Cathedral body there are certain persons appointed, I suppose, for no other reason except on account of their proficiency in preaching. Whether it is desirable that "the six Preachers" should continue as heretofore to address merely a scanty number of persons on certain week-days, or be called upon to address more numerous congregations at other times, it is for you who manage the affairs of the Cathedral to consider. Also I would ask whether there is not something unreal in the idea which has so long prevailed throughout our Cathedrals, that no man as a general rule should be invited to preach in a Cathedral unless he is a member of the Cathedral body. Certainly the examples of St. Paul's and Westminster, and I believe Durham and Chester, seem to point in an opposite direction. And whatever may be your particular views as to the best mode of obtaining this object, you will agree with me that we ought in such a place as this to endeavour to secure the services of the best and most able preachers whom our Church numbers amongst its Ministers. Now, I would venture to suggest that many persons may be most eminently qualified to hold high posts in our Cathedrals without having the peculiar gift of which I have been speaking, and it is certainly our duty to find for every man within our Cathedral body that occupation which is best suited to his peculiar talents and the peculiar training he has had before he came to be a member of that body.

Our Cathedrals, however, are not merely places for the worship of God and the preaching of the Gospel. We must not forget that they have always been, and I trust they will continue to be, homes for learned men. Run through the roll of those who by their works have adorned the theological or other literature of the Church of England, and you will find that almost every distinguished name is connected with some one of our Cathedrals. I trust that this peculiarity of our Cathedral bodies will never be interfered with. We do require in this busy age places where men may live, quietly following the daily worship of the Church and refreshing their studies by its divine service as celebrated day by day. We do require that sort of hallowed leisure which has been so productive of great men in the Church of England in past times, and which, I trust, will ever continue to provide such ornaments of the Church.

Moreover, our Cathedrals are doubtless intended to be the centres of the dioceses in which each of them is placed. In most Cathedrals, as in this, that connexion with the diocese is kept up by the presence of the Archdeacons in the Cathedral body; and certainly I should be very ungrateful if I did not say on this occasion that probably no Cathedral in England is so intimately connected with the diocese in which it is placed, as this Cathedral is through its Archdeacons. During the time when, by God's dispensation, I have been little able to discharge my diocesan duties, I have had the satisfaction of knowing that in every deanery the Archdeacon has been present to assist and help in the work that had to be done. I have had the satisfaction also of knowing that through the revival (in consequence of my illness at first, but not solely on that account) of the ancient office of Suffragan Bishop in the person of a member of your Corporation, a new life has been breathed into the work of this diocese, and I believe that no Archbishop that comes after me will be able to dispense with that great assistance.

I should be sorry if any arrangements which in future might be made with reference to our Cathedrals were so to tie your body to the diocese as to cut off connexion with our ancient Universities or with the metropolis. Still, I think it is well worth your consideration, whether those who are necessarily living here for a considerable portion of each year might not be more distinctly enlisted in some work connected with the diocese than our existing system has allowed. I am not one of those who think it very desirable that our Canons should all reside here during the whole year. I confess, having weighed that matter very carefully, I think more good is done by their bringing us into connexion with other places in which they reside during some portion of the year. But still I should be glad if we were able to present to the Church the distinct sight of some connexion between diocesan work and the tenure of a canonry in this Cathedral. I am aware of the great practical difficulties which from time to time seem to stand in the way of the improvement I have now suggested, but I do not think these are insuperable, and I believe that if it were understood that each canonry had some sphere of diocesan work assigned to it, those whose business it is to select Canons would have regard to the particular work which the possession of the canonry implied, and this without diminishing that connexion with the Universities and with the general life of the country which we think it so important to preserve. I have ventured to suggest these matters for your consideration because they are very much in men's minds in the present day, and because I believe that there is scarcely any change of this kind which we are not competent to make of ourselves. I do not think that any revolutionary changes are at all required in our Cathedral system. It is merely needed that we should work heartily and well to fulfil the ideal which we all propose to ourselves. And if any real difficulty be found in the necessary relaxation of the existing statutes and usages, we ought to seek for the powers required.

I do most earnestly trust that the Cathedrals of the Church of England will maintain their great position as long as England itself lasts. Who can doubt that in past times they have done great service to the Church and nation? We do not require to go back to the old days when they were centres of missionary enterprise for the district in the midst of which they were placed. I believe that in every age, according to the lights and wants of that particular age, they have served many purposes for which they were originally founded—changing, no doubt, but essentially the same; their old buildings carrying us back to mediæval antiquity and uniting us with the Church of the past; their learning uniting us with the Church of all ages, and the gatherings within their walls to hear the Word of God preached reminding us that the peculiar wants of the peculiar age in which we live may be met by our present members, as well as the wants of the past have been met by those who before occupied their places. I trust, I say, it may please God that these great institutions be preserved, and that all of us who are gathered here to-day, old and young, will do our part in making them instrumental for the promotion of God's glory. We have all marked with pleasure the beautiful and costly restorations which have been made of late years of the material fabric of so many of our noble Cathedrals. Where such works are not yet completed, they are now almost everywhere in progress; as for example at Wells and Rochester, under their present able and zealous Deans. And we are all in good hope of soon seeing St. Paul's beautified in a manner befitting the central church of the capital.

We must not forget that the Cathedrals are also great places of education. The presence of so many young faces here to-day reminds us of this. This King's School is a place of great importance, not only for Canterbury and Kent, but it has a reputation also in England, and we shall not any of us forget that we have duties to the rising generation,—duties which, I am thankful to believe, are now and have for years been faithfully performed by those who preside over this Cathedral.

Neither should we forget that these places are intended as centres of charity, and that it was the desire of those who founded them, by gathering together some of the indigent around us and connecting them with the Cathedral, to make us ever remember that one great part of our work is in our Master's name to attend to the welfare of the bodies and souls of our poor.

III.

(Delivered at Canterbury to the Rural Deaneries of Canterbury, Ospringe, Westbere, and Sittingbourne, October 3rd.)

My Reverend Brethren, and my Brethren the Churchwardens:

I am anxious to bring before you to-day some matters which very intimately concern us as members of the Church of England by law established. It is not unusual in the present day to hear men state that there are great difficulties in our position in virtue of our being an Established Church. I believe these difficulties—not generally seen by the laity, and only by a small portion of the clergy—will be found, when we examine them carefully, to disappear.

It is somewhat difficult to give a definition of an Established Church. In those famous lectures delivered by Dr. Chalmers many years ago in London, which had the effect of stemming the tide of public opinion at that time, the lecturer dwelt upon this characteristic of an Established Church—that it was an endowment for the teaching of the Christian religion to the nation. There are other things supposed by some to constitute more truly than its endowments the essence of an Established Church; as, for example, that the ministers of the Established Church have a mission to the whole nation. It is not true that any one of our parish clergymen is fulfilling his duty, if he looks only on those with whom he has more intimate sympathy, and not on the whole of the people committed to his care. He is bound to consider that the whole parochial area which is assigned to him is the field of his labour, and that all who dwell within that field are entitled to receive, as far as they are willing, his pastoral ministrations. No doubt there are in other countries established churches of which this is not the distinctive mark; for example, in Belgium the system is that all religious bodies are recognized by the State, and receive pay from the State for the performance of their duties, and therefore all may be considered as in some degree established. That, however, is not the custom which has ever existed in our country. Now, this point of our having a mission to the whole people in virtue of our being ministers of the Established Church lays us under very great and grave responsibility; and I trust that there is not one amongst the clergy here present who is not imbued with a sincere desire to accomplish this mission, knowing that according to any mere congregational system a vast number of the poor come to be altogether neglected, and that if the ministers of our Church are not ready to succour them in their spiritual and in their temporal needs, they run great risk of being neglected altogether. Indeed, in such a state of society as that which we see around us in this age, when vast masses of population are gathered together in our towns, beyond the ordinary means of grace, it must follow that unless the clergy of the Established Church consider themselves as distinctly responsible for the outcast poor, those persons will have no pastoral superintendence.

According to the system of supply and demand which exists in non-established churches, there will be no demand on the part of the outcast poor, and therefore no supply of religious ministrations on the part of the ministers of the various denominations. I do not deny that the ministers of other denominations will exert themselves in a missionary spirit, and that they will do and have done in times past much good among the outcast poor, but this is not their especial office as it is ours, and the responsibility, therefore, is heavy indeed upon us to see that no poor person, under any disadvantageous circumstances, is excluded from the benefit of those ministrations which the Established Church of England calls upon us as its ministers to afford. I do not think, then, as far as we have gone hitherto, we can consider that there are disadvantages attending our position as ministers of an Established Church, though there are great difficulties and responsibilities.

But I desire now more particularly to dwell upon one point in connexion with our peculiar position, which has caused very considerable difficulty to many conscientious persons, especially among the clergy, and which it is well we should calmly consider. I will not discuss to-day, but reserve for a future occasion, the supposed difficulties which an Established Church finds, in the way of exercising its legislative functions; that is, altering or improving from time to time any of its formularies or the regular order of its system. I wish to call your attention to-day not to the legislative but to the judicial part of this question. It is commonly stated that there are very great difficulties attending the position of an Established Church in the administration of its ecclesiastical laws; and I wish that we should quietly and calmly examine whether there really are such difficulties or not.

Now, in the first place we may grant, that when the Lord Jesus Christ founded His Church upon earth, and gave His written word to be the law according to which it was to be administered, propounding the great principles by which all ecclesiastical law was to be arranged, the Church's judicial functions had at first to do with purely spiritual matters. The ordinary administration of justice in common courts of law had then very little place for interference in such matters. And no doubt when as time goes on we find ourselves encumbered by the necessary conditions of our mixed existence, and are continually coming athwart questions not purely spiritual, but partly spiritual and partly concerned with matters of this world, it is not unnatural that men should be disposed to fret against any interference of the powers of this world with the administration of matters spiritual. But a little consideration will very soon convince us that such is our mixed condition of existence, that it is impossible practically to separate the one from the other; and the moment men have fully recognized the principle that he who preaches the Gospel ought to live of the Gospel, and that it is the duty of those who appreciate the Gospel to provide funds for its diffusion— the moment this is recognized, there steps in a new element not perfectly congenial with the purely spiritual element, and there arises the necessity for the intervention of the common civil power in matters which otherwise might have been reserved entirely for the decision of the spiritual authorities. Now, I wish that this shall be distinctly understood. The moment that there is property of any kind, the civil courts must in some degree intervene. Is this, then, a difficulty which attends only the Established Church of this or of any other country? Are there not endowed bodies of Dissenters amongst ourselves, and is there not a great Roman Catholic body which has large endowments? And the moment any difficulty arises as to their endowments, the possession of their edifices, or the sustenance of their ministers, I am here to maintain that these bodies, having no distinct connexion with the State, become as much amenable to the decisions of civil courts as any Established Church that ever existed.

I wish to recall to your minds one or two facts which may illustrate this point. Probably it may be in the memory of some of you, that in a very remarkable speech made by Sir Roundell Palmer in the House of Commons not very long ago, he distinctly stated this—that he had been employed by the Baptists; that he had been consulted by them upon this question of law, whether or not communion with the Baptist body depended upon having received baptism—that is, whether an adult who, according to their system, had delayed his baptism, was entitled to be considered a member of their community; and as I understand it, that eminent lawyer gave his opinion on this question, which otherwise would have come before the supreme civil courts to be decided—and that question, touching closely on theology, would have been debated before the civil courts—namely, what is the exact position in which the baptism of an adult stands to the rules and regulations of the Baptist body? Now, I will give you another instance. You are aware that in the Church of England difficulties are felt regarding our connexion with the Privy Council, because the Privy Council decides in matters which have reference to doctrine. This is felt by some to be an unwarrantable interference of what they regard as a civil court, even when the two Archbishops of the Established Church and the Bishop of London sit in the Council to assist the judges in their decisions. Now, I happen to remember that not very long ago there was a dispute in the non-established Presbyterian body in South Africa, and the question was this—whether a minister who had professed a doctrine which the majority of the body to which he belonged condemned, had really gone beyond the limits of what in that body was considered to be allowed? Now this question came up to the Privy Council as a matter of appeal, because the minister, though belonging to a non-established Church, had demanded of the civil court of the colony, that he should be replaced in the position from which he contended he had been unjustly removed. As you probably know, an appeal from the colonial courts comes to the Privy Council, and the Council therefore (without, of course, the assistance of the prelates), acting in a purely civil capacity, decided the question. Unless I am mistaken, the decision was that the clergyman in question had not transgressed what were supposed to be the doctrines allowed by the body to which he belonged (though I believe he had denied the personality of the Tempter), and therefore he was to be replaced in the post of which he had been deprived. I may give you another example. There is at this moment—though it may not be known to many of you—a dispute in the Free Church of Scotland. Certain persons, it is alleged, wish to deviate from the doctrines which were laid down as the basis on which that body was originally founded at the time of their secession from the Established Church, and the persons who entertain these wishes are the majority apparently of that body. The minority are strongly opposed to them; and I understand they have distinctly threatened the majority that if they persist in their present course the minority will appeal to the civil courts, to ask whether these particular views which they maintain to be part of the essence of their original constitution, are part of that constitution or not.

My opinion is very strong, with these three instances before me, but it would be as strong without them, that no set of men in this country, whatever denomination they may belong to, can altogether free themselves from the dominion of the civil courts in the decision of questions which intimately concern their confession of faith; because wherever property is concerned the civil power must decide whether there has been any violation of the rights of property, and whether or not there has been any departure from the original contract under which property is held. I know no way by which this can be evaded, except one, which, I believe, has been adopted in some instances—namely, that every person who becomes a minister or office-bearer in any particular community shall do so under solemn promise that he will never appeal to the civil courts to vindicate his rights. I believe there are bodies in which such a promise is made. I confess I consider such a promise absolutely wrong. I consider that it is setting up an *imperium in imperio*, such as the laws of England ought not to recognize. I consider where this has been done there is a complete handing over of the individual office-bearer, be he minister or be he layman, to the absolute will of the majority for the time being.

Now, it may be asked, if it be true that this difficulty with regard to the intervention of civil courts must affect all religious communities, how comes it that we have more of the intervention of such courts in matters connected with the Established Church than in other bodies? Well, there may be many answers given to that question. One would naturally be this: that our body is spread throughout the whole country, and numbers, even according to the calculation of those who are most opposed to it, as many members as all the other bodies put together. This may be one reason why we hear so much about legal questions in the Established Church. Another reason may be this—that it holds a higher position socially, and therefore attracts more attention. Another may be that it has, and I am thankful that it has, fostered amongst its people more of the spirit of freedom, and that no person who is a member or office-bearer of the Church of England thinks that he has to be the slave of a majority, or that he is to be put down merely by those who happen from time to time to have authority over him; but thinks that as he is a freeborn Englishman, so he is also a freeborn member of the Church of England, and entitled to be judged by its laws. I do not think this is a bad sign of the Church of England, but the contrary.

Moreover, there is another reason why we hear more of such cases in the Established Church than in other bodies; namely, that the parish priests of the Church of England, according to the constitution of our Church, have a freehold in the position which they occupy. Some may say, "This is bad; it is one of the very things we complain of." And no doubt it is one of the things which cause us difficulty, but it might be a fifty-fold greater evil to get rid of it. For suppose the clergy had not this freehold in their offices. What is the alternative? They must be subject to the arbitrary will of some one. Of whom? If we go to France, we see to whose arbitrary will the priests of the once free Gallican Church have been reduced to be the slaves. Few clergymen in France hold their office except at the arbitrary will of the Bishop, and that is not what the clergy of the Church of England desire, if I am not mistaken. Well, if they are not subject to the arbitrary will of the Bishop, perhaps they would be subject to the arbitrary will of their congregations. I do not think the clergy of the Church of England, with all the respect they have for our lay members, would feel comfortable if they were liable to be dismissed, as soon as their congregations objected to their teaching or their mode of conducting divine service. Nor do I believe our laymen have such a desire to exercise tyranny over the clergy. My conclusion therefore must be that, notwithstanding all the difficulties attendant on our system, nothing better can be suggested than that the clergyman shall retain his freehold without disturbance except by judgment of law.

Now, if I am right in my view of this whole matter, I wish to ask this further question, whether there be not some advantages which the Church of England as an Established Church possesses over other bodies which are not established, in respect to its relation to Courts of Justice? I believe we shall find that a great characteristic of the Church of England as an Established Church is this: that as it is an Established Church the courts of the Church are recognized as courts of the realm. Other bodies, when any difficulty arises as to property, or as to whether a man is straying beyond the limits which the system of his community has laid down, are obliged to go to a purely civil court; but it is of the essence of our Established Church that there is no necessity for this, because, according to our constitution, the ecclesiastical courts are courts of the realm, and their decisions are as binding as the decision of the Queen's Bench or any other civil courts. The Bishop's Court, which in any non-established body must be a mere private court of reference, becomes a court of the realm. To the Archbishop's Court there is a regular appeal by law, and its judgments have binding force as the decision of a court of the realm. And when we rise beyond the Archbishop to the Queen in Council, I do not know that we have any right to say that we have left ecclesiastical courts to go into the civil court.

The fact is that a very old dispute must be considered in reference to this matter. Long before the Reformation the sovereigns of these realms claimed that in all causes and over all persons in these their dominions they should be supreme, and that the last appeal should be to the sovereign, even from those courts in which jurisdiction is exercised distinctly in the name of ecclesiastics. The only period during which this was not the case was when such appeals went straight to Rome. We know that the sovereigns of these realms before the Reformation contended strongly against the right of the Pope to draw appeals to Rome, and at the Reformation these appeals to Rome ended. What, therefore, was the natural consequence? Why, of course, that these appeals having been taken from the Pope were to go to those from whom the Pope had unjustly drawn them in the first instance; and hence, accordingly, as a matter of history, whether we approve of it or not, between appeals going to Rome and appeals being decided by the Sovereign, there was really no other course left. That course was adopted which was sanctioned by the custom of the country. Now, I suppose, as none of us wish to go to Rome, we must be satisfied with a decision according to the authority of the sovereigns of the realm. As you are aware, such trials of appeal came, after the Reformation, to be conducted in the name of the Queen in a department of Chancery. You are aware, in all probability, that there was a court called the Court of Delegates, which heard these appeals; that the sovereign appointed persons, many of them laymen and some ecclesiastics united with them, whose business it was to hear these appeals; but that this system of the Court of Delegates was found to be inconvenient. You are aware that some thirty years ago a commission was issued to inquire into the whole matter; and the result of this commission was to remove these judgments in cases of appeal of this kind from the Queen in Chancery to the Queen in Council. It is sometimes said that it was by a mere accident that cases strictly ecclesiastical were consigned to the Privy Council; but I believe that a candid examination of the reports made by the Commissioners who were appointed to investigate the question, and to the Acts of Parliament in which those reports were afterwards embodied, will prove that it was by no accident whatsoever, but most deliberately, that these cases, being taken from the Court of Delegates and the Queen in Chancery, were transferred to the decision of the Queen in Council. And in order that there might be careful attention to matters strictly ecclesiastical in cases under the Church Discipline Act, care was taken that in such cases the Archbishops of Canterbury and York and the Bishop of London should be members of the Judicial Committee of the Privy Council, in order that they might advise the civil judges who sat upon it.

Now, I am not here to say that this is the most perfect court for deciding such questions; I am not here to say that the Queen's Bench is a perfect court; I am not here to say that any court in existence has attained perfection; and I am not here to say that this court should not be reformed:—but I do say that so long as it is a court we are bound to obey it, and I say we shall be very negligent of our duty both as English Churchmen and citizens if we allow our private feelings to stand in opposition to the law of the Church and the land. We shall do despite to our holy calling if we set up our own arbitrary will against the calm decision of a court, which, whatever may have been said of it, I think will be allowed to have shown itself in recent cases very impartial in the way in which it has administered justice to all parties who have come before it.

But, my brethren, on a future occasion I hope to enter more at length into some of the difficult questions which have arisen from the decisions of this court. At present I have spoken merely of our necessary connexion with the civil power from the fact of our having property to dispose of, and of the peculiarity which characterizes our position in reference to the civil power in our being members of an Established Church. And I am very much mistaken if on full and serious consideration of this matter you do not come with me to the conclusion, that on the whole we have little to dread from the interference of the civil power in causes ecclesiastical, and that we receive greater benefits from our connexion with it than are possessed by any other religious body either in this or in any other country.

But, having touched upon this matter, and endeavoured to lay before you what is our position in reference to the judicial decision of questions which from time to time arise in our Church, let me, before we part, most earnestly beg you to consider what is the duty of a Christian man as to obedience to the law under which he is placed.

In addressing a large and thoughtful body like this, of clergy and laymen, it would seem almost ridiculous to dwell upon the duty of obedience to the law, and I do not believe amongst the persons to whom I am now speaking there is anything but an infinitesimal minority that would dispute the duty of obedience to the law of the Church and of the land. And when we speak of the law of the Church, I wish it to be understood that no man is entitled to say, "I myself will interpret the law of the Church." Neither civil society nor ecclesiastical society can hold together if every man, in spite of the decision of the judges, is to lay down for himself what he considers to be the law. I believe there are very few clergy who will differ from my views on this matter; but there may be a few, and we live in an age when a very few persons, by making themselves very conspicuous and talking very loudly, are able at times to persuade the community that they, a small minority, are really a majority. And therefore the mischief which may be done even by a few persons acting in a lawless and insubordinate spirit, taking upon themselves to interpret where they ought to listen to authoritative interpretation, may greatly injure the Church. I trust, therefore, that all who are tempted to do so will consider with themselves that it is un-Christian thus to act, and that no man placed under authority can justify it. I must charge the few clergy who, in this diocese, are in the habit of doing so, hereafter to abstain from introducing into the services of the Church anything which they know has no place in the Prayer Book or in the Articles, or from taking on themselves in doubtful cases to decide what is lawful in the Church of England. No desire for unity with other bodies will justify any clergyman in adopting such a course.

Do not let it be supposed that I wish that we of the Church of England should be tied hand and foot in the bonds of a narrow uniformity. Look at the services in this Cathedral and compare them with those in some ordinary parish church, and you will find both of them strictly abiding by the law and custom of the Church of England. Here is diversity enough, but yet there is essential unity. But those to whom I allude are not satisfied with this wide range, and are determined to introduce from foreign churches practices which have no justification either in the custom or in the law of the Church of England. I most earnestly charge them to be content with that liberty which the Church of England allows, within the limits of which there is ample room for great diversity in the midst of a loyal unity. But if on the one hand, in matters of doctrine, we try to include persons who are not believers in Christianity at all, or on the other hand persons who have abjured their allegiance to the Church of England, and are looking to a foreign church to which to give their allegiance, we destroy all essential unity, and our diversity would very soon end in complete destruction of the body to which we belong. But I have little fear that there is danger of destruction from such a cause as this. The Church of England is wide, and I am glad it is, for if it were not it would not be Catholic. The Church of England has existed ever since Christianity was founded on these shores, altered indeed in external form, purified and reformed three hundred years ago, and even in those three hundred years there has been great and natural diversity of opinion and yet the same essential unity. With this diversity, which is not inconsistent with essential unity, we may well be contented.

I knew two Bishops of the Church of England who died a few years ago. One was my contemporary and friend, the other my pupil. They were both members, as it happened afterwards, of the same cathedral chapter; both were called to the highest posts of the Church of England; both were struck down in a remarkable manner by sickness, and cut off in the prime of life, but not before each in his Master's cause had performed signal services to the Church of which each was an ornament. Walter Kerr Hamilton and Samuel Waldegrave were as different as any two men who were both attached members of the Church of England and thorough Christians could be. No two men could take more diverse views of the great theological questions that divide us, or have more dissimilar tastes as to ritual. But each of them was a father in Israel; each left his mark on the diocese over which he faithfully presided; each was revered and honoured as a saintly character. Attention was drawn to the lesson to be learnt from their case in a consecration sermon by my friend the Dean of Durham, three years ago, when each had been prematurely cut off by a mysterious blow. Each loved the Church of England, each was faithful to his trust in his own way, and according to the convictions of his own heart, though their convictions were in many respects diverse. But they had that essential unity which consists in the love of their common Lord, in the belief of His eternal Deity, in the deep conviction of their own lost state by nature, and of the absolute necessity of His atonement to wash away their sins. And who that knew them doubts that they are now united before the throne of God? Let us be content with this unity which belongs to us all; and if we are diverse in the expression of our feelings within the proper limits which the law allows, no one will find fault with us, and we shall each be better able to do our work, because we work conscientiously as in Christ.

Another name occurs to me, of one differing from both of these—a name known and honoured wherever the English tongue is spoken, as a faithful minister of Jesus Christ and a great reformer in this land—Thomas Arnold. Who will venture to say that he was not a faithful minister of the Church of England? And yet his convictions were very different from the convictions of these two Bishops. This is the sort of width as to opinion and practice which it is wise to allow in the Catholic Church of England. The Catholic Church of England, which, in its Ritual as in its teaching, was wide enough for these, may well satisfy us. We are not tied to a dull, over-strained uniformity of thought and worship, but we can allow no unauthorized eccentricities borrowed from a foreign system. The few who would drag us into these extremes will do no good to themselves, and I am quite sure they are not acting faithfully to the Church.

But let me for one moment press this upon you: That the sort of questions with which we have been dealing to-day may withdraw us from the more important question: How are we each striving in our several places to fulfil our deep responsibilities?

As to my brethren the Churchwardens,—some of them have stated that they have great difficulty in performing their duty, and that in consequence of recent legislation, which has altered the right of collecting money from church-rates, their churches are not in the good order in which they desire to see them. Let me impress upon them the absolute necessity of taking some steps for the full performance of their duties. It is the condition of all of us from time to time to find ourselves in a new position in consequence of alterations in the law: our business is, of course, as soon as possible, to adapt ourselves to that changed state of things, and to find some substitute for what has passed away. Now, with regard to the maintenance of our services and churches in proper order, two modes may be suggested: one is to levy a voluntary rate, which will no doubt be readily paid; and the other is to have offertories in the churches, appropriated to the purposes which church-rates formerly served. It will not do to say that the law is altered and that therefore everything must take care of itself. That the law is altered, this is the very reason why we should exert ourselves and see that some substitute is provided for that which by the action of the law has been taken away from us. I thoroughly believe that the laity of the Church of England are determined not to allow their churches to fall into ruins or their worship to be conducted in a slovenly manner. Before another visitation, some mode will be found, which, by appeal to the voluntary allegiance of those who love their Church and are ready to advance its interests, will fully supply the lack of that which has disappeared. The duties of the churchwardens in this matter are plain, and they are important, and they bear very much upon the maintenance of religion. Without these outside signs that our religion is flourishing, inward and spiritual religion will suffer loss. I fear that the heart of religion will be injured if injury befall the churches which are the enduring ornaments of our land.

To my brethren the Clergy, let me say before we part, that as to all the questions which may engage our thoughts, no inquiry is so important as this:—Am I, in the sphere in which God has placed me, discharging my duty and responsibility to the flock of Christ? Am I attending to the poor? Am I teaching children in my schools? Are my sermons week after week the utterance of my heart to the hearts of my people? Do I study as for my life the Gospel which is the charter of their and of my salvation ; and am I determined, God helping me, that the Church of England shall at all events have this strength—that it has in my person a godly, self-denying, and persevering minister? If so, if this spirit spreads amongst us, our Zion is secure. Nothing can ever prevail against the Church if its ministers and its people are faithful to that Gospel which He sealed with His blood.

IV.

(Delivered at Canterbury to the Rural Deaneries of Bridge, Elham, Sandwich, and Dover, on October 4th.)

My Reverend Brethren, and my Brethren the Churchwardens:

I endeavoured yesterday to bring before those who were here assembled, some thoughts on the administration of our ecclesiastical law in the Church of England; and the conclusion to which I desired to lead their minds was this, that no individual scruples or dissatisfaction with the law could justify anyone in acting in a disobedient spirit, where the proper authorities of Church and State had spoken without any doubt as to what was the duty of a clergyman of this Established Church of England. We saw, when we were examining this matter, that though the law, having been now several times invoked in cases which have occupied much of recent attention, had laid down with tolerable precision what things were not lawful in the Church of England, still there was a wide field for those differences of sentiment and even of practice, which, in the midst of essential unity, have always more or less characterized this National Church; but that there were limits beyond which the law had explicitly stated that no one should go. And I stated then, what I gladly and honestly repeat now, that I believe the loyalty of our clergy is such, that they are quite ready to yield obedience to the law of the Church and the State within these limits; and if there be here and there one or two persons who claim for themselves a liberty which the Church does not allow, I cannot but trust that their good sense and sober consideration of the matter will ultimately bring them to a better mind. And I feel confident of this, that the public opinion of the Church is against all self-willed innovations which individuals take upon themselves to make against the declared authority of the Church. You will easily understand that I do not consider it a part of my business, nor do I consider it to be the business of the Bishops who preside over the Church generally, to act in any inquisitorial spirit as to the conduct of the various clergy who are placed under their charge. This, however, I have no hesitation in saying, that I do believe it to be the duty of the Bishop, if any complaint is regularly addressed to him, to examine into the matter carefully; to consider with himself whether or not there has been a violation of the law; to reason in the first place with those who may have been misled into any such violation; and in the last resort, if he finds it impossible to compass by persuasion the end which it is his duty to promote, then to exercise that authority which devolves upon him as a chief magistrate of the Church. You will not, I am sure, suppose that I am for a moment forgetful, how dangerous it would be to excite men's minds to a narrow criticism of everything which takes place in every church within our diocese—how unwise it would be to infuse suspicion into the minds of the laity, and set them watching every minute gesture of the clergyman in the discharge of his sacred duties. I trust that we are none of us forgetful that things may change, and change for the better, even though at first those who are the witnesses of the change very much dislike it. It is impossible for anyone to have arrived at my time of life and to look back upon the state of parish churches some thirty years ago—to remember the walls damp with mould, the careless way in which the communion table was treated, the bad psalmody and worse instrumental music which used to be heard in many of our parish churches, to remember the very few who used to gather round the Lord's table as compared with the hearty bands of worshippers who gather there now, and the general improvement in the whole externals of our worship which has been brought about I must say principally through the instrumentality of one section of the clergy,—it is impossible, I say, for any man of fair mind to look back upon all this, and not to allow that changes may occur which are, at first, unpalatable to those who witness them, and yet, after a course of a very few years, are recognized to be extremely useful, and conducive to God's glory. But while we allow this fully, it is plain that here, as in the points which we noted yesterday, there must be a limit; and if there be a tendency anywhere, as undoubtedly there is in some quarters, to push matters to an extreme and to introduce practices not sanctioned by the law or custom of the Church, and which savour of an uneasy hankering after a foreign and less pure system of religion, then it is only natural that the laity should consider themselves aggrieved by the introduction of such practices, and it is the duty of the heads of the

Church carefully to watch that no excess arise which shall alienate the laity and destroy the purity of our reformed worship.

Now, having said thus much—a recapitulation in some sort of what I said yesterday—and having reminded you that the limits within which a clergyman is confined in these matters are now tolerably explicit; and having pointed out, I trust with sufficient clearness, to the churchwardens, that as they are the officers of the Bishop, it is their business, in case of their seeing anything introduced beyond what they conceive the law allows, to communicate with the Bishop or Archdeacon, after having first talked the matter over in a friendly way with the clergyman;—having, I repeat, stated all this with reference to mere ceremonial, I turn to-day, in connexion still with the administration of ecclesiastical law, to another matter which requires a somewhat different treatment.

You are all aware that a very distinct decision was pronounced last year as to the practices which were to be allowed in our ceremonial worship, and many practices which were gradually creeping into some parishes were pronounced to be illegal. Another case has since that time arisen which has to do, not now with the outward ceremonial of religion, but with the doctrines which it is lawful to preach from our pulpits. But, before I enter upon the particular case to which I have alluded, let me say a few words as to the general rule which those who administer the law of the Church of England in such matters seem to have laid down for themselves during the last twenty or twenty-five years, to guide them in their decisions. As I said yesterday, the Church of England is intended to be a National Church. It is not intended to be in any sense a sect. It is a Catholic Church, embracing in its teaching all the great Catholic truths which have been witnessed to since the days of the Apostles. It is also a National Church, including persons of very various minds, according to their various circumstances, and the various education and training which they have received. The history of the Church of England, carrying us back to the age of the Reformation, presents peculiar features. In the days when Popery disappeared from high places amongst us, the very difficult task devolved upon the Sovereign and her advisers of constructing a system which was to embrace the whole English nation. If it is difficult even in the present time to bring men to accord, with differences of training and of natural character, how much more difficult this must have been at a time when the traditions of many centuries were so distinctly at variance with the new light which had burst upon the world with the Reformation! Those, therefore, who had to conduct that most difficult experiment were bound to make the limits of their Church as wide as might be, in order, if possible, to embrace the whole English people. Hence we should naturally expect that though the great men who lived at that time had distinct convictions as to the essentials of the system which they were about to present to the world in opposition to that which had so long darkened its horizon, yet they were very anxious, and very justly anxious, not to magnify into a matter of primary importance anything on which it was reasonable and right that freedom of opinion should be allowed. Some scoff at the Service Book of the Church of England and its

Articles as if it were a mark of some failure or insincerity in its leaders that it allows this diversity of opinion. I, for my part, consider it to be greatly to its glory that the Church which is presented to us is no sect, but a branch of the Catholic Church as well as a body accommodating itself to the varying sentiments which must arise amongst earnest and godly men in a nation like ours, accustomed to freedom. Now, such being the case as to the original compilation of our formularies,—and our Reformers having, as I thoroughly believe, acted in full accordance with principles which had come down to them from the time of the Apostles,—for the difference of character in the different Apostles, as is now granted I think by all who have carefully studied the New Testament, was not without influence upon their mode of presenting the one truth of which they were the heralds,—I say, our reformers having wisely adopted this system, what has been the result in the Church of England? We who live in this generation, and look back upon the time of comparative deadness in which our fathers lived, rejoice to think that the Church of which we are members was wide enough to admit Simeon and Wilberforce. Those who in their day, in spite of much opposition, held forth the great evangelical truths which had for a time been overlaid or overlooked, never thought of leaving the Church of England, but found within its formularies full scope for the preaching of that Gospel in its purity which their hearts loved. When we look still further back we have no reason to regret that the Church of England was able to lead the van, in the struggle against Deism and various forms of infidelity, under such men as Paley; and if we look back to the time of Archbishop Tillotson, we do not, I think, regret that the Church of England found in its formularies sufficient room for men of his turn of mind. When we look back further, I suppose there is not one of us who would wish that George Herbert or Bishop Andrewes should have been cast out of the Church of England. Therefore we enter upon this question with a distinct conviction that the Reformers, when they made our formularies such as they are, were wise. The result has been that, amid all the fluctuations of opinion and of the history of the country for the last 300 years, this Church, with its formularies such as I have described them, has a strong hold over the great majority of the nation: it is loved and honoured by persons who under any other system might have been separated one from the other, whereas the experience of 300 years has shown that they are able heartily to co-operate under the guidance of those formularies. Now, with such views before them, what is the duty of those who are called upon to administer the law of the Church of England in matters of doctrine?

I suppose most who are here present remember what is called the Gorham Case. I am not going to trouble you with entering upon the question which in connexion with that case was raised before the highest Court of Appeal; but I am just going to remind the juniors amongst you of the trembling anxiety with which the decision of the judges was awaited: how anxious most of us felt that no judgment should be pronounced which should in any way restrain the liberty of the great Evangelical party, or declare that their common mode of interpreting the formularies, and especially the Baptismal Service, was not fairly admissible within the Church of England. We remember also—those of us who are old enough—not only the anxiety with which the judgment was awaited, and the relief which was felt by so large a body when it was pronounced, but also the cry of dissatisfaction with which it was received by many; the threats—in some cases unfortunately carried into effect—of secession from the Church, and the general attempt on the part of extreme persons to represent that the Church, because it was wide enough to include, honestly and fairly, the great Evangelical party, had been unfaithful to its trust. That time passed away. Another case came before the same tribunal of a very different character. The questions now raised had no longer anything to do with the Sacrament of Baptism; they had to do chiefly with the doctrine of the inspiration of Holy Scripture. All of us —for it is but a recent matter—remember the anxiety felt by many in that case. However little sympathy men might have with the persons whose case was brought before the court, there was great anxiety lest there should be such a decision on the subject of inspiration as should go beyond the wise limits which the Church had hitherto maintained. Well, there was a decision, guarded and wise, as I venture to think, on that very intricate question. I do not know that any evil has followed from that decision. Men see as clearly as they did before how the Church of England maintains the majesty of Holy Scripture; how it tests every doctrine by its accordance with Holy Scripture. They have as readily as before prized as one of its noblest features that readiness which the Church of England has always shown to open the Bible to its people and invite them to study its pages as the charter of their salvation. I see no symptoms that the Bible is less thought of among those who highly prized it before, and the danger was avoided of defining with scientific accuracy the nature of God's influence upon the hearts of inspired men, and so of our Church substituting a mere human dogma in place of that free acquiescence in the guidance of the Holy Spirit which has been sufficient for Christians of all ages who reverence God's Word, without inquiring too minutely as to the exact mode in which God caused it to be uttered. I think that was a wise decision, and no harm happened from it. What, then, do I think of the latest decision which has caused so much alarm in the Church?

Now, first, I would call your attention to this fact, which is characteristic of all the three cases to which I have alluded. The judges have in each made this the basis of their judgment, that it is not their part to settle what is the doctrine of the Church of England; that the doctrine of the Church of England is clearly settled and laid down in its Articles and formularies, and that their business is merely this—when a man in a penal case is brought before them, and the question is whether or not he is to be punished, to settle whether he has so flagrantly transgressed the law that he ought to receive condign punishment. Now, let us suppose for a moment that this were not a case of theological speculation or teaching, but one of morality: let us suppose for a moment that a man were brought before the Supreme Court charged with some act of immorality; that it was found he had gone very far, but that he had not actually gone beyond those limits within which a charitable interpretation might be put upon his conduct, and that therefore the decision of the court was that he should not be punished. Would any man in his senses say that the court which came to this decision had decided that the immorality of which he was accused was of no importance? The question is—Has the particular person who is accused in this instance so flagrantly transgressed the limits of the law that the court feels it cannot give him the benefit of the doubt, and therefore cannot, without swerving from the maintenance of the law, allow him to go unscathed? That I consider to be the exact issue which in all these cases is brought before the court. I, therefore, cannot understand that anyone can maintain that, because in the particular instance in point a certain theologian has been acquitted, therefore the law of the Church of England has been altered. It should be remembered, that the court had only a few months before declared in the most formal manner that those ritual acts which seemed to symbolize the doctrines of which this clergyman was accused were altogether illegal. This also ought to be remembered, that in the particular case in question the statements made by the person accused had been modified by himself; because he was told by his friends that if his work went forth in the form in which he had published it, it was impossible but that a fair tribunal must find him guilty. I think, therefore, that an escape under such circumstances does not give any ground for our believing that the particular practices and doctrines which were brought before the court at the trial have been declared in any sense to be the doctrine of the Church of England, but that we are referred for decisions of what our Church of England doctrine is to the whole Articles and the formularies of the Church. And so the sole question in this case, and in all such cases, has been—Has the person who is brought before the court been found to have so completely transgressed the law that it is impossible to give him the benefit of a doubt in his favour?

At the same time, of course it is quite impossible to shut one's eyes to this fact—that it is a wide view of the doctrine of the Church of England on which all decisions on these matters have for the last thirty years been based; and, as I have already stated, I conceive such width is consistent with Catholic usage in the best sense of the word, and with the traditions of the particular Church to which we belong. I am not going to maintain that there ought to be room for every man in the Church of England for whom there is room in heaven. Of course there are points, some even not of primary importance, on which if men differ it is impossible that they can be united in the same outward communion. All who know the history of the discussions of former ages, to say nothing of our own, grant that it is totally impossible to have in the same Church persons who cannot do with Bishops and persons who cannot do without Bishops: if one man holds Presbyterianism of Divine authority, and another thinks it most important that Bishops should exist, of course there must be separation. If one man holds that infants ought to be baptized, and another that they ought not, it is a very difficult matter indeed to suppose that they can be united in the same outward communion. But still it does seem to me that the ideal of our Church is this— that men who agree in the grand essentials of Christianity, who reverence the Lord Jesus Christ in His

Divine nature as our Lord and Saviour, who look to His purifying blood as the atonement for their sins, who confess themselves to have no hope of salvation without His death and passion, who point to the written word of God as the test by which all our doctrines are to be tried—such men should, as far as possible, be united in one communion, and I trust that as men become earnest in the great duties of their calling they will more and more realize such truths. Those who wait as faithful pastors by the beds of the dying will come to think less than in days of carelessness of the divisions which keep men asunder; and the lay brethren who see their clergy labouring heartily for the good of Christ's people, showing in their self-denying lives that they are animated by the influence of the Holy Ghost, will not be very captious in watching their peculiar modes of worship, or their peculiar opinions on less important points. We are all soon to stand before the Judgment-seat of Christ, and the questions which at that great award will be settled for us will have little to do with the differences which separate Christians on earth, but will all refer to those great Gospel truths through belief in which we hope to enter into the enjoyment of our Lord's presence.

V.

(Delivered at Ashford to the Deaneries of North and South Lympne, and East and West Charing, Oct. 7th.)

My Reverend Brethren, and my Brethren the Churchwardens:

I endeavoured at Canterbury on the two last days of our visitation to bring before the clergy and churchwardens some thoughts on the condition of the Church of England as an Established Church in reference to the administration of its ecclesiastical law. I wish to-day to turn to another subject, on which it is still supposed particular difficulties attach to the Church of England from its being an Established Church—I mean our ecclesiastical legislation.

It is sometimes said that we are bound hand and foot by our connexion with the State, so that we are quite unable to accommodate ourselves to the changing circumstances of the changing ages through which the Church of England has to minister. It is said that the system which is thus rigid and immovable is altogether unfitted to deal with the wants of the great Christian community. I wish that we should examine this question quietly and calmly to-day—how far we in our particular position as an Established Church are under any peculiar disadvantages as to ecclesiastical legislation.

Now, I would first remark that, looking to the nature

of the Church of Christ and its duties, it does not seem desirable that there should be a system of incessant change going on in its organization. The truths which we have to communicate from age to age are one and the same, and no variety of circumstances can justify any alteration of that Gospel which, once for all, was delivered by the Lord Jesus Christ and His Apostles, and which can know no change. But even with regard to other matters we are not to take it for granted that it is a very desirable thing that change should be easy. Indeed, I know of no system in any of the non-established branches of the Church in other lands, which are in full communion with our own, in which greater facility is given to change in their formularies and constitution. And I think it is worth inquiry whether in other religious bodies, when changes have been made, considerable difficulties have not followed. The Nonconforming bodies have exhibited to the world in the course of their history a perpetual tendency to split into smaller sections, and I suspect, if you examine these splits in Nonconforming bodies, you will generally find that they have arisen from some change which the majority have forced upon the minority, and the minority has had no means of defending itself except by separating from the body which has overruled its will.

But turn to another body very differently situated from the Nonconforming communities. We have heard a great deal within the last few years of changes in that which has hitherto claimed to be unchangeable; and those who have watched the condition of things in Italy, in France, in Germany, and in our own country, may be inclined to think, perhaps, that the attempts to introduce great changes in the Church of Rome have caused very great difficulties, which a more quiet and consistent adherence to things as they were might have avoided.

Having laid down this principle, that upon the whole we are not to desire great and rapid changes in the system of the Church, yet still, I am free to confess that, to meet the varying circumstances of our community, certain changes must from time to time be required, and I wish to know whether the Church of England has exhibited to the world a peculiar inability to make them when necessary. There are many of us old enough to remember the very great changes which occurred in relation to the system of the Church of England some thirty or forty years ago. I am not going to recapitulate the alterations which the wisdom of Archbishop Howley thought it right to sanction in the system of our Church: the restraining of non-residence and pluralities, the alterations of limits of diocese, and various other matters.

But let us rather look at things which have lately come under our own immediate observation.

It so happens that, during the time in which I have been privileged to take part in public affairs, there have been some important changes. We remember a certain deadness and unreality which used to be felt at our public worship on the 5th of November. We felt that the "State services," as men named them, had outlived their day, and did not call forth that grateful recollection of the events which they expressed, nor that degree of religious feeling which it is desirable should pervade the congregations assembled on such solemn occasions. Well, somehow or other, by a distinct act of those in authority, these State services have disappeared, all except one, which I am sure there is no clergyman or layman present this day who would not desire to see retained—the service in which we pray the blessing of Almighty God upon our gracious Queen on the day on which she ascended the throne.

But other changes have also been legitimately and regularly made within our memory, which most of us will agree are good, and which were really not very difficult to attain as soon as people had made up their minds that they were desirable, and were ready to face the slight difficulties which stood in the way. Those who began life at the time I did will remember that there was a superabundance of oaths and declarations which met men on their entrance into office, civil or ecclesiastical. They will remember that a good deal of opposition was from time to time expressed as to the very rigid words in which adherence was declared to the Articles and formularies of the Church. Many thoughtful men could not be reconciled to the old mode of expressing their adherence to those formularies, a mode which had been originally adopted at a time when those in authority were desirous, if I may use the word without offence, of being revenged upon the Puritan party, who had ejected them from their livings a few years before. It was naturally felt that the very rigid terms in which men declared their assent and consent to all and every the words of the Thirty-nine Articles and the Prayer-book went a little beyond what was really necessary for those who were to be faithful ministers of the Church of England. Hence, as the legitimate and constitutional mode of remedying the difficulty, a commission was issued, of which I had the honour of being a member, with the late Archbishop of Canterbury and the Archbishop of York and many other eminent and learned dignitaries of the Church, as well as laymen of great authority. The result was a recommendation that these modes of subscription should be relaxed. The matter, as was right, was submitted to Convocation, and, as the time had come when the Church was ripe for change, Convocation at once assented. A bill was brought into Parliament, and the terms of subscription have been changed. Now I think no one who has considered our relation to bodies external to the Church of England, or to the rising thought of the country, will hesitate to allow that this was a salutary change; and the moment men recognized that it was a thing to be desired, the supposed difficulties in the way of doing it disappeared. I doubt whether other bodies have been as ready to adapt their forms of subscription to the wants of the age as we have. I suspect if you examine the matter you will find that in other communities very antiquated declarations are still made with reference to heresies, the very existence of which is scarcely retained in the memory of those who make the declarations. However that may be, at all events we had little difficulty in placing ourselves in accord with what the voice of the Church and the nation considered to be necessary for the times in which we live. Again, in 1871 was passed the new Table of Lessons' Bill, founded on a report of the Ritual Commission, in consequence of a generally expressed wish.

Now I turn to another matter, which is of yet more recent occurrence. Most persons have felt that, with the vast change in the population of this country, the mode in which great masses of workmen grow up in particular

neighbourhoods, uninstructed in the Church's system—
through whose fault it is needless to inquire—it is very
difficult to bring that full and well-regulated system of
the Church's worship, which, when drawn up, was intended for its well-trained and well-disciplined members,
to bear upon the wants of such populations. Hence there
has been a growing desire that the system of the Church
of England should become somewhat more elastic, in
order that it might meet such cases as this. In the
diocese of London I heard a great deal of such cases, but
we hear of them in other places, in large rural districts,
as well as in places like this, where the railway has ac-
cumulated great numbers of labourers. Well, has any
great difficulty been experienced in finding a remedy?
As soon as people were convinced of the necessity of
bringing forward the change which was required, the
ordinary process, according to the constitution of our
Church, here also was adopted. The Queen issued her
commission to the Archbishop of Canterbury, the Bishop
of London, and various other Bishops, to various learned
divines from the Universities and elsewhere, as well as
to various laymen known to be interested in the spiritual
welfare of their fellow-citizens. The result was, that
meetings of the Commission were held, and in course of
time a report was made. It was laid before Convocation; Convocation approved it; the matter was embodied
in a bill and laid before Parliament, and before the end
of last session—having been only introduced at the
beginning—this bill became law. It seems, then, that
many of the difficulties as to necessary changes in
the Church of England, of which we have heard so

[1] See Appendix D.

much, were difficulties which consisted in two things: first, in men making up their minds as to what changes were really desired; and, secondly, when these changes were settled as desirable, in other persons making up their minds to have the boldness to propose them.

As I have entered on this subject, let me now call your attention to the changes which have thus been made, the greatest which have been introduced in such a matter since the time of Charles II., which would not have been introduced in the formal way in which they were, unless it were intended that the clergy should carefully consider how far it is desirable in each parish to use the liberty now granted. Let me, therefore, as shortly as I can—not to weary you—point out what is the liberty that has been given. First, with regard to the daily services. No one can doubt that there are in all town parishes, and often in country parishes, persons to whom it is a great blessing to have daily access to their parish church, in order that they may invoke God's blessing upon the labour of the day; but there are few people who will not agree with me that experience has shown how difficult it is to gather together any large congregation of hearty worshippers in the midst of the busy occupations of men's lives in this age. The law which has recently passed has enabled the clergy to accommodate the daily services to the wants of their people, and I think every clergyman will be naturally expected to consider carefully in his parish how far this new system opens to him opportunities of Common Prayer which were denied to him before.

Now I turn to the second point. In town parishes, and in most parishes where there is anything like a large population, I am thankful to believe that the zeal of the clergy has not confined their public ministrations to the two stated services which the law requires. Now it was felt, and very justly, that the repetition three times a day of the same service was not, upon the whole, the system of worship most conducive to edification; and hence, during the last session of Parliament, on the recommendation of the Commission and of Convocation, power was given for the introduction of a third service, which should vary from the others.

Again, we have felt that special occasions arise in every parish when it is desirable that there should be special prayers differing from the ordinary service in use at the ordinary time. Such liberty of introducing special services for harvest festivals, or on an occasion of any great sudden judgment which happens to visit a neighbourhood, or for any other remarkable occasion, is now sanctioned by the authorities of the Church and State.

Again, it was felt that there might be in many of our parishes, especially in towns, difficulties from the length of the services; that the very great length of three hours or more for services when the Holy Communion was administered, was not, on the whole, conducive to edification. Hence it was distinctly sanctioned by the legislation of last session that, in cases where it was found desirable, services might be divided. Many held that this could lawfully be done before, but doubts existed, and it was thought best to have a distinct assertion of the legislative authority both of the Church and State, that there was nothing irregular or belonging to any peculiar sect or party in this dividing of the services.

Again, it was felt that in great towns, round our Cathedrals and other great churches, there were many persons living who might be attracted by preaching, but who are very little accustomed to the ordinary services of the Church of England. It was thought that there could be no harm, but a great deal of good, in drawing them into our churches that they might hear what we had to say, and thus making our churches more available for the preaching of the Word of God. I repeat, therefore, that as these changes have been made, we are all bound in our several spheres to consider how far it is desirable that we should avail ourselves of the liberty thus given.

I have spoken hitherto of the changes which, as a matter of fact, have been introduced. I believe also that there is no great difficulty in introducing others as soon as it is recognized by the Church generally that the time has come for them to be desirable. For of course, if we have made some which prove to be beneficial, we shall naturally consider whether there are any still before us. Far be it from me to penetrate into the unknown future. I believe we shall find that the mode in which alone such changes can legitimately be introduced is a safeguard against any rash innovation; and, at the same time, that wherever changes are really proved to be necessary to the Church and nation, they will be introduced.

I must not, however, fail to mention one other great and important change with reference to one of the Creeds, which has been very much in men's minds during the last few months, respecting the desirableness of which there is, in many minds, great doubt. You are aware that the moment it was considered right that a commission should be issued for the consideration of all the rubrics, those who knew the past history of men's minds felt perfectly convinced that it was impossible longer to delay a full inquiry into the question as to the retention of the Athanasian Creed in our public services. Those who look back some thirty or forty years remember the discussions which had arisen on that subject then, and those who are acquainted with the history of the last century know that these discussions were not new. If other matters have for a time drawn away public attention during the last thirty years from this subject, still I think we must all be aware of the difficulties which have often stood in the way of young men entering upon holy orders, and that the general feeling of the country has been that whenever the rubrics were to be examined, this question of the Athanasian Creed, among others, would have to be considered. Therefore the Commission of which I have spoken did not avoid this subject.

First, let us ask whether there was any real difficulty which it was necessary that the Commissioners should discuss. With regard to the declaration of the Athanasian Creed on the subject of the doctrine of the Trinity, all members of the Church of England are, I believe, agreed; but that the minute logical statement of the particulars of this doctrine should be rehearsed in public worship, on this there has been legitimate diversity of opinion. All of us agree that the hopes of our salvation depend upon the Three Persons in One God. It is not the declaration of this doctrine that has caused difficulty. It is chiefly the statement of what are called the damnatory clauses. Now all of us who have subscribed to this Creed know that there is some explanation which prevents these clauses from having the full force which they appear grammatically to have.

I am not very much concerned as to the antiquarian questions about the origin of the Creed, or at least with their bearing upon the matter now before us. But one point all are agreed upon; that is, that the Creed was not written by the Apostles, nor by any infallible or inspired authority, and therefore, as the work of man, it stands in a totally different position from the inspired Word of God, and the mere antiquarian question does not affect the point which is now before us. If our friends, in the University of Cambridge or elsewhere, are enabled to throw any light upon the earliest Manuscripts, of course we are very grateful for their assistance. But still the plain question is this: Is it desirable that this Creed, with what are commonly called the damnatory clauses, should continue to be recited twelve times a year in the services of the Church of England? On the one hand it is urged that the Church dares not conceal the stern denunciations of God's judgment on unbelief, set forth by Christ Himself, and by St. John; while on the other it is pleaded that, in announcing these judgments, we have no right to be more explicit than the Lord Himself, and that the great divine truth, which the damnatory clauses imply, suffers, rather than gains, by its human adaptation to a specific form of teaching.

· It is granted that this Creed is not used in the public services, as we use it, by any other Church. It is admitted that the Greek Church repudiates those statements which contravene its own peculiar doctrine denying the procession of the Holy Spirit from the Son. We, in these days, have been brought near to the Oriental Churches; we have been visited, for example, by an Oriental Archbishop, who was welcomed in our homes, and in some of our churches. I have more than once been called upon, by those who have authority in the Church, to put myself in communication on important matters with the Patriarch of Constantinople, thereby acknowledging him and his brethren as Bishops of an orthodox Church. I pronounce no opinion here as to the errors into which the Greek Church may have fallen, but many have urged with great force the inconsistency of thus addressing its chief pastor, while we continue to use habitually in our service words which would naturally appear to him to declare that he and all his people shall without doubt perish everlastingly.

In the Ritual Commission this question was discussed, and a proposal was made to the Commission by an eminent layman of this diocese (Earl Stanhope) to the effect that in the rubric, which directs its use, the word "may" be substituted for "shall." The Commission came to the conclusion that it was not wise in that stage of the matter to allow this alternative to the clergy. It was then proposed that a rubric should be introduced, similar to that sanctioned by the Commission of 1689, to the effect that the damnatory clauses are only intended to apply to those who wilfully reject the catholic faith. Since that time another explanatory rubric has been suggested, which has received the assent of Dr. Pusey and the other Divinity Professors at Oxford, to the following effect; that the condemnations objected to do not apply to anyone who, through involuntary ignorance or invincible prejudice, refuses to assent to the catholic doctrines. I have lately met with another explanatory note, mentioned by my revered friend Dr. Moberly, Bishop of Salisbury. He, while himself desiring the total omission of the damnatory clauses, calls attention to a proposed explanatory rubric, stating that God's threatenings are to be understood only as they are generally set forth to us in Holy Scripture.

None, however, of these proposed explanatory rubrics has met with general acceptance, and many persons think that words which require so much explanation had better be omitted.

On the whole, opinions have now generally come round to what was at first rejected in the Commission, viz. that an option should be allowed as to the use of this Creed, and the Archbishop of York and myself have been addressed by a large body of laymen, recommending this course.

It is well to remember that the practical solution of this question may be far more difficult than many think. I know that much obloquy has been cast upon the Bishops for not having given their own opinion, and for having rather thrown the burden of the discussion upon the Lower House of Convocation.

Now I beg you to remember that there are two questions—one, what is the best course in itself, and the other, what alteration is feasible under the circumstances. On the first of these questions most of the Bishops, I believe, have expressed their own opinion, in some public way, as to what they think best to be done. Certainly I have expressed mine in the most explicit manner, viz. that the best plan would be to remove the Creed from the regular services of the Church, and to retain it in the Articles, for I hold that it is quite legitimate to declare, as we do in the Articles, that the Creed may be proved by most certain warrants of Holy Scripture, while we maintain that the Creed itself is separable from the anathema which accidentally accompanies it.

I trust we may arrive at a satisfactory conclusion respecting the second question. I believe I could myself acquiesce in any one of the suggested alterations, all of which I consider to be, on the whole, preferable to the existing state of things. But now I must state, though with much reluctance, that the greatest difficulty in the way arises from the unreasonable conduct of certain eminent persons, who declare that they will break the Church in two, if we adopt any other than their own particular way of settling this grave difficulty. Such conduct, I say, is deserving of our reprobation, and I trust that, after full consideration, those who are guilty of it will come to a better mind. All of us are anxious to maintain the great doctrine of the Trinity, and that there shall be reality in our declarations; and if we meet with a great difficulty, which has long pressed on the minds of earnest men, we have a right to seek the best advice, and to request these learned and devout members of the Church to assist us, and not to commence the discussion with an unwarrantable declaration that they are prepared to break the Church in two if the decision arrived at does not meet their own particular views. But, after all, I trust it may be possible to settle the matter. A very large committee of both Houses of Convocation of the Province of Canterbury will soon meet, and endeavour to arrive at a satisfactory conclusion. The Archbishop of York and myself have promised to give our most serious consideration to the subject, and, if we can, we shall endeavour to relieve those who declare that they suffer under a grave difficulty. We shall consult, as we are bound, our brother Bishops and the clergy generally, our anxious desire being to modify the rule as to the use of this Creed, if it can be done consistently with the maintenance of truth and of the peace of the Church.

There are other questions awaiting solution which have been treated of in the Report of the Ritual Commission. Amongst them stands the difficulty which many of the Clergy state that they have found in the indiscriminate use of the Burial Service. When the Church comes to consider this or any other question that may arise, let us not doubt that God will be with us to guide us. If changes be found to be really desirable, then He will be with us to show us our path.

And now let me end with this solemn word of admonition:—

I have been speaking of the outward forms and organization of the Church. These are things of which we can all take cognizance. But let it not be forgotten that the first mark of the Church which is mentioned in our Creed is its holiness. It is "the Holy Catholic Church." This is a mark concerning which each of us is bound before God to examine himself unceasingly, and no questions of mine can search your spirit. I commend you to God and to the word of His grace, beseeching you to remember that if the Church be not holy it is none of His, that if its priests be not holy, they cannot be its faithful pastors, nor win souls to be partakers of its Lord's holiness. The words of the Head of the Church still remind us that as "Men cannot gather grapes from thorns nor figs from thistles, so cannot a corrupt tree bring forth good fruit." May this lesson abide with us, that the clergy of the Church of England may bear forth to their congregation that witness which the priests of the ancient Church of God bore upon their foreheads continually, " Holiness to the Lord ! "

VI.

(Delivered at Sevenoaks to the Deaneries of Shoreham and East and West Dartford, October 17th.)

My Reverend Brethren, and my Brethren the Churchwardens:

On other occasions when we have met on this visitation I have spoken chiefly of matters concerning the outward constitution of the Church. I desire to-day to turn rather to some points concerning our ministerial faithfulness. It is well that the outward machinery of the Church should be rightly arranged; it is well that if there be anything lacking it should be supplied; but after all it is on the mode in which we one by one acquit ourselves in the duties of our ministry, and avail ourselves of the machinery with which our Lord has supplied us in His Church, that the safety of the Church of England depends, and by our faithfulness to this that we ourselves shall be tried.

Many of you, I am sure, must have been struck last Sunday with the words of the First Lesson when it was read in church.[1] They certainly seemed to me very appropriate for a visitation; and if you will allow me, I will read a few of them now:—

"Son of man, prophesy against the shepherds of Israel; prophesy, and say unto them, Thus saith the

[1] Ezekiel xxxiv.

Lord God unto the shepherds; . . . The diseased have ye not strengthened, neither have ye healed that which was sick, neither have ye bound up that which was broken, neither have ye brought again that which was driven away, neither have ye sought that which was lost.

"Therefore, ye shepherds, hear the word of the Lord; Thus saith the Lord God; Behold, I am against the shepherds; and I will require my flock at their hand, and cause them to cease from feeding the flock; neither shall the shepherds feed themselves any more."

Thanks be to God, the chapter, taken as a whole, is a wondrous exposition of His love and tenderness. The greater part of it is the announcement of His care for the sheep, an encouragement to shepherds who seek to be found faithful, as well as a warning to those that are selfish and negligent. What higher comfort can you have in your daily work for the welfare of the poor than remembering that God is working with you; that He Himself hath said: "Behold, I, even I, will both search my sheep, and seek them out. And I will set up one shepherd over them, and he shall feed them, even my servant David: he shall feed them, and he shall be their shepherd. And I will make with them a covenant of peace."

I do not suppose that the warning words which I have quoted apply only to those whom we are in the habit of calling "Pastors." They apply to all who hold any office, pastoral or other, in the Church of Christ. They apply to civil rulers, and to all who have any influence which they can use for the good of men's souls; and therefore, while I trust that their severe reproof is not addressed to any of you, certainly they contain for us all a most solemn warning.

A visitation ought to be a time for us all of much searching of heart, I trust also of much spiritual refreshment. The Great Shepherd of the sheep on this occasion puts to you, to me, to all, the searching question, " Are you faithful according to the means which I have given you, in feeding my flock?"

I have issued a great number of questions, which to some of you may seem almost too minute, on the subject of the condition of your parishes. I hope carefully to peruse the answers, and where necessary I will communicate with you, by writing, on the matters you suggest. And now, leaving general questions respecting the condition of the Church, let me address myself to a few of the distinctly practical questions which a visitation ought to bring before us. I shall dwell first on the mission which is assigned to us as ministers, each of his own parish. No degree of external activity can compensate for the neglect of that which is distinctly committed to you, each in his own peculiar sphere. Each man must begin with the discipline of his own soul. Next, let him order well his own household and family, through which untold influence may be exercised over the parish of which he is the centre. Let these matters therefore pass in review before us now.

The Church of England, in its parochial system, possesses peculiar means of influence, there being a minister in the centre of every parish, and a parsonage in almost all cases, the residence of the clergyman's family. Let each of us, then, look well to our own personal influence and the influence of our families. Let each of us take account not only of the direct work which we are doing, but of the indirect influence which flows from our homes. The clergyman's family is dear to the Church of England. We rejoice to be a Church the clergy of which live in family life. And the mention of this reminds me that in this diocese there is a society very intimately connected with the families of our clergy, the society which provides for their widows and orphans.[1] Its rules are simple and good. Prizing family life, you will not neglect to provide for those who are dear to you, for it is of great importance that in the uncertainties of life you should do so, as much as you may, in case any sudden blow comes upon you. I commend that part of our diocesan arrangement to your careful attention. No doubt many of the laity would be glad to assist this society, for they know how inadequate are the means of the clergy, with the many calls upon them, to provide for their families, and I believe that the laity only need to be called upon to give their ready assistance in this very important matter.

But turning from your own families and your own private life, let us now think of your public ministrations. Let each one ask himself what is the condition of that house of God in which he ministers. Are all outward things so arranged in it as to tend to the edification of Christ's people? Is the building in good order, decently furnished and arranged? Are the services of the Church so ordered that all your people

[1] See Appendix E.

may benefit by them? Many matters of detail might here be alluded to. It is sometimes complained that merely such a matter as the reading of the service requires greater attention than it has hitherto received. In other professions in which a man has to come forward in public, if he does not acquit himself well in his public ministrations no one employs him. But the clergyman has in this matter a sort of monopoly, and is therefore bound to see, by his own watchfulness, that there be in his peculiar mode of reading the services nothing that shall be an offence to his people. This may seem to some of you a matter of small importance, but it is not, and it is well that the younger clergy especially should guard against any habit which, however trivial it appears, may be a real impediment in the way of the success of their ministry. I would also ask what is the number of services in our churches. Do we take care that there shall be services at such times on the Lord's Day as are most suitable for the peculiar wants of each parish? Do we take care that all the adjuncts of those services shall be so arranged as to conduce most to the edification of our people? Are our churches closed from one Sunday to another, or do we take care that the spirit of those enactments of our Church which require that the house of God shall be often open is not neglected in our case? I think a man acts somewhat thoughtlessly who allows, for example, the various Saints' Days which have been appointed to be observed, in order that great truths might in regular succession be brought before the minds of our people—I say, I think a man acts unwisely who allows those days to pass without any mark. It may be a matter of discretion what service you will have—whether you will have it in the evening, or whether you will have the regular morning service—but under any circumstances I do not think it will be wise to allow the Saints' Days to pass unheeded.

Efforts have of late been made to revive the observance of Ascension Day. Let me express my earnest hope that a day to which the Church attaches such great importance that a Special Preface is appointed in the Communion Office, will henceforward be always, duly observed.

Arrangements, as you know, are now made for giving greater facilities to the people for public worship, by shortened services. I have spoken of these elsewhere, and only remind you of them now in order that you may avail yourselves of the opportunities which they offer.

And now I come to the great ordinance of preaching. What makes a good sermon? A great many things go to the making of a good sermon. Nothing so much as this, that we should speak from the heart to the heart. A dull discourse, which does not speak the real sentiments of the preacher, which does not try to search the conscience of the hearer, certainly will never come up to the idea of a good sermon. Much reading is required of the clergy, especially in these days, when all men read, and when the clergy, who are teachers, cannot, with safety to their cause, be behind those whom they teach. There must be reading of all kinds —reading of ordinary literature—but, above all, regular and careful "reading of the Holy Scriptures, and all such studies as help to the knowledge of the same." No man who is to do his duty in the preaching of the

Gospel can neglect such studies. But, after all, there may be the utterance of the fervid spirit, there may be the results of much reading; but for your preaching to be effectual, there must be added to these things the speaking forth of the experiences of your own spiritual life. If a man does not himself understand and appreciate the spiritual truths of which he speaks to others, his voice will be to them but as the sound of "one that can play well upon an instrument," and will never reach the heart.

And then what is to be the matter of our preaching? All other subjects sink into utter insignificance compared with the one subject of our Lord Jesus Christ. An essay, however ingenious, however learned, however it may go through the great truths of morality, and cull from all sides illustrations of the importance of those truths, will altogether fail of doing Christ's work unless He Himself is the main subject of the whole of it. Christ in all His offices, ministering to the wants of His people, Christ dwelling amongst us in His human nature, giving Himself a sacrifice for our sins, raised to the Father's right hand, and perpetually making intercession for us, yet evermore present with His people now, according to His own most holy promise—this must be the sum and substance of our preaching if we are to reach our people's hearts. But the preaching of the Sunday will have little effect unless it be followed up by private ministrations. A parish is neglected if the various persons living in it are not distinctly aware that they are continually under their pastor's eye, and that their wants are known to him. Hence the necessity of a subdivision of large parishes, that no one may be left out in a crowd; but that, going from house to house, the pastor may be felt to be the friend and guide of old and young within the whole limits of his parish. No doubt there are great difficulties in doing this. How are you to reach the working men? They are not to be found at home except at unusual hours. How are you to reach the lads who are disposed to break off from the discipline of the school, of which they are tired? All these things we have to lay carefully to heart, and everyone is bound to ask himself what effort he is making to overcome these plain practical difficulties, which stand daily in our way. In every well-regulated parish the clergy will not work alone. Did we say that it is a great blessing to have a family in the clergyman's house? No doubt through the family influences will be extended over classes which otherwise could not be reached. And we must call in the assistance of our lay neighbours. Every clergyman who works his parish well must have a large staff of persons on whom he can depend to assist him in the visitation of his people; otherwise, however active he may be himself, I fear he must leave some unattended. Now, you are aware that in London a great movement was made lately for the establishment of a society of lay assistants, and the numbers who have now joined that society are very great indeed. I remember that at the time when the Bishop of London's Fund was originated, a demand was made for five hundred additional voluntary lay assistants. I do not know that that number has been reached, but a large body of lay assistants have associated themselves together.[1] Hitherto in this diocese, though some slight progress has been made in this work of lay

[1] See Appendix F.

association, it has only been here and there, and I trust that before another visitation comes round, there may be, as suggested by Archbishop Longley, a large body of lay assistants associated together in this diocese. And while you visit your people one by one, and attend both to old and young, you certainly will not neglect the duty of catechising the young. This matter is so important that it has found a place in our rubrics. Confirmations have been greatly multiplied in the diocese of late years, mainly through the untiring exertions of the Suffragan Bishop. Last year there were eighty confirmations in Kent.[1] We used to think sixty a large number in the great diocese of London. You will not, I trust, fail to appreciate the importance of drawing the young members of your flock to Confirmation, and of seeing that they be duly prepared and diligently instructed. Certainly at no time was this ever more important than now. I am not prescribing when or where this catechising is to take place, but, as things now stand, if our children are not carefully taught through our instrumentality the value of the formularies of our Church, they will not learn them at all, and a vague and indefinite system will take the place of that regular training in the doctrines of the Church of England which has hitherto been maintained in all our schools. Every faithful clergyman will therefore now, more than he ever did before, determine that, God helping him, he will attend to the specific and regular religious training of the children in our schools.

But the Church of England does not confine its work to the regular routine of that sphere to which each of us is appointed. We do our work best, perhaps, within

[1] See Appendix G.

our own particular sphere, if at the same time we are ready to go beyond it. Sympathy grows by its expansion, and those who are most laborious in their regular parochial work are also most ready to co-operate in the general mission work of the Church. Now it is a great mistake to suppose that all our mission work has to do with people at a great distance. Many of the parishes from which the clergy and churchwardens have been summoned to-day touch the metropolis, and the very same difficulties which prevail in the metropolis also prevail in those parishes adjoining, in which the population is growing so rapidly that the ordinary means of grace cannot penetrate the mass. There are many labourers coming down from the great metropolis into the adjacent villages, and going up daily to their work, whom, if the clergyman does not seek in a missionary spirit and by some distinct missionary efforts, he must leave altogether neglected. It is a good and hopeful sign of the times that our churches in such districts are now often used for missionary services.

There are other parishes in this diocese presenting very peculiar features, besides those which adjoin the metropolis. Our long line of sea-coast has many towns in which a population grows up with very peculiar characteristics. Those populations of seamen—and some of those towns are also military stations—present great difficulties. The clergy who work in those parishes will not fail to make every possible missionary effort to reach those who are abandoned and outcast, whom, if they neglect, no one will care for. You are aware that there exists in this county a Penitentiary Institution at Stone, and that several self-denying women have associated themselves to rescue the outcasts of their sex.[1] Many, by God's blessing, have thus been rescued. In all large towns, especially in such places as those I have alluded to, there ought to be a house of refuge, and the clergyman of the parish ought to see that the home or refuge is rightly managed, and that the claims of the outcast body are brought regularly before his people. Assuredly the Lord Jesus Christ, who in the course of His earthly life was ever ready to reclaim those who had fallen, and to bring back those from whom others, priding themselves on their own uprightness, were ready to turn aside, will look with favour upon every devoted act by which we now endeavour to rescue our fallen 'sisters. Once more let me return to His gracious words in the chapter I have brought before you already to-day:—"As a shepherd seeketh out his flock in the day that he is among his sheep that are scattered; so will I seek out my sheep, and will deliver them out of all places where they have been scattered in the cloudy and dark day."

But there are, close to our homes, other fields of distinctly missionary work beyond the limits of our parishes. I am glad to see here to-day the chaplains of our workhouses. I trust that those to whom this most important charge is committed will most faithfully watch their opportunities of fully accomplishing their work; and I trust that any of our lay brethren who are here to-day, and who in their office of guardians are called to select chaplains for our workhouses, will remember that there is scarcely any position more important or more difficult properly to fill than the chaplaincy of a workhouse. To give the smallest conceivable salary, and take the

---

[1] See Appendix II.

first man that offers, will be a great neglect of duty. Remember how arduous and difficult the work is. Be ready to give a proper remuneration for most important services, and select as before God the man whom you deem best fitted for some of the most difficult parts of Christ's work. The chaplain of the workhouse has to deal with those whose former life very often has unfitted them for easily receiving religious impressions. He has to deal with the most outcast and abject. It is his duty to see that the young are rightly taught; that they have been baptized, and that they be brought, as far as his exertions will extend, to Confirmation. He must watch that old age is soothed in its decline, and that those who go forth from the workhouse are not neglected. He will not do his duty well unless he watches over the girls who leave the house, and see, as far as he can, that they are provided with suitable employment. And seeing how very difficult this part of his work is, he certainly requires every encouragement and help which can be given him by the laity. In London and elsewhere, ladies have associated themselves, with the full approval of the guardians, to visit in our workhouses, and the most beneficial results have followed; persons leaving the workhouse, who otherwise would have been altogether lost, have been helped to live a consistent and useful life. I trust, therefore, that all of us, both clergy and laity, will remember this most important mission of the Church of England.[1]

I have spoken of the great difficulties of reaching the

[1] Besides those who actually enter the workhouse, there are in every large parish orphan children whom a little assistance rendered in time may rescue. For such we have now our Diocesan Orphan Home, which I earnestly commend to attention. (See Appendix I.)

working classes who are gathered together in our villages and towns; but time would fail if we were to enter on a full consideration of the machinery which we ought to organize in our parishes to reach the working classes. I may say, however, that a clergyman is not rightly fulfilling his duty who does not endeavour to have some institution in his parish, a reading-room or a lecture-room, whereby the men who are growing every year in intelligence may find that that growing intelligence need in no way separate them from the influence of the Church.

There is one dreadful evil overspreading the whole land which makes havoc of thousands of our working men—the evil of intemperance. This is one of the practical matters to which Convocation has addressed itself. A committee was appointed to examine into this subject of intemperance under my friend the Archdeacon of Coventry, and results of the labours of that committee have been embodied in a report which has already received wide circulation, and I believe has done much good. I commend it to your most serious consideration. It is the bounden duty of every clergyman to see what efforts can be made in his parish to bring men to an understanding of the misery of drunkenness. I say not to what association you ought to join yourselves, but this I do say, that unless you make distinct and positive efforts against intemperance, you will be neglecting an evil which is eating out the very heart of society, destroying domestic life among our working classes, and perhaps doing greater injury than any other cause which could be named in this age.[1]

[1] See Appendix K.

These few hints will suggest to you practically how much distinct missionary work there is, besides the ordinary mission to our parishes, which each of us has received from our Lord and Master. But a man does not rise to a sense of the full responsibilities of a clergyman of the Church of England, who does not continually remember that it has a mission far wider than our own land. In every well-regulated parish there will certainly be some effort to stir up interest in missions to the heathen. One or other of the great Societies will be brought particularly before your people's minds. It is proposed to observe the 20th December next as a day of special Intercession for an increased supply of Missionaries.[1] Some persons suppose that in this age, heathenism, like vice itself, may be robbed of all that is bad in it, provided it be refined and varnished over with a thin coat of civilization. I do not think that is the view which either you or I will take of our duties to the heathen. The Lord Jesus Christ has charged all of us to spread His Gospel throughout the world; and Churches will be judged by this, whether they have taken their part in that great work; and each individual Christian, and especially each minister of our Church, who neglects his duty in the matter of missions to the heathen, will certainly not escape the condemnation of the Lord to whom their souls are dear.

But, my friends, we might stay here all day thinking of various matters on which, at the time of a Visitation, we have to examine ourselves as to our practical faithfulness to our trust. Let me once again ask each of you to take himself seriously to task. Let the

[1] See Appendix L.

Visitation be the subject of our individual prayers, that we may learn, each of us, better to estimate the degree in which we are fulfilling our responsibilities. The Church of Christ needs a godly clergy and a godly laity; godly Christian homes amongst rich and poor; vigorous efforts made by all to reach those whom Christ has committed to them; farmhouses and large mansions sanctified by family prayer; a general interest in the work of Christ; and this general interest leading us to see His image in the men and women and children around us: an interest in the value of souls, beginning with our own persons and our own homes, extending then to our own parishes, and spreading thence through our whole country, and from our own country to distant colonies and the most distant parts of the earth. The man who wishes to know whether he is answering to his responsibilities as a clergyman or lay office-bearer of the Church of England, will pass all these needs in review before his mind, and ask himself serious questions as to each. Do they say the Church of England is in danger? No doubt it is. As long as the powers of evil are busy in the world, there is danger for the Church to which Christ has committed the great work of resisting the powers of evil. But where is it to seek for its defence? In the hearty, godly, Christian profession and practice of its members. On all of us individually, on the way in which each fulfils his responsibilities, far more than on any outward supports, far more than on any admirably adapted machinery, does it depend that the Church of Christ shall do His work, and the Church of England remain taking its full part in that work till time ends.

VII.

(Delivered in Tonbridge Church, to the Rural Deaneries of North and South Malling, November 5th.)

My Reverend Brethren, and my Brethren the Churchwardens:

We are now approaching the end of this Visitation. I have thought it well to-day, at our last meeting, to address to you a few thoughts on this subject—the relation in which the Church of England stands to other religious bodies, both at home and abroad.

I do not think that this subject will be unprofitable for those lay members of the Church who are here in an official capacity to-day. It is well for us, both clergy and laity, to examine carefully the position in which our Church stands in Christendom; and though possibly some here present may not entirely agree with the views which I wish to bring before you on this subject, still I think it will do all of us good carefully and calmly to consider the matter; and you will not refuse to give due weight to what I lay before you.

Five years have now passed since Archbishop Longley assembled at Lambeth a great gathering of the Bishops of the Anglican Communion throughout the world. At that time there were many—not unnaturally, for almost every measure of the kind was sure to be objected to—who felt objections, and stated them, to the course which he pursued. But I believe that, in an age which rather delights to magnify differences than to draw men together in the Christian Church, Archbishop Longley adopted a wise course. He assembled our Bishops from all quarters of the globe, and thus exhibited before the world the greatness and extent of our Church, and showed how those who preside over its remoter branches are able to co-operate with us at home in the spirit of love, and thus he gave an answer to many who are disposed to represent the Church of England as so divided that it is impossible for its ministers to act heartily together. From China, from the Cape of Good Hope, from New Zealand, from Canada, from our brethren in Scotland, from our brethren in the United States of America, and from Ireland, was gathered together that great assemblage at Lambeth. The result of our deliberations was, I think, very satisfactory. Some matters of detail with regard to the mode of carrying on the discipline of the Church were carefully talked over and arranged; and there issued from that body a Pastoral which had this characteristic,—that it set forth, solely and simply, the great Gospel doctrines in which the Church of England rejoices. We added, and attempted to add, nothing to the Creed and Articles which we had received from the Lord and His Apostles and those who followed faithfully in their steps both before and at the time of the Reformation; but a simple statement went forth of what, in the belief of the members of the Anglican Communion throughout the world, were the great Gospel doctrines which all of us accept. And I think that that statement, though there was no novelty in it,—for the subject admitted of no novelty,—was a valuable document, as showing how we of the Church of England hold fast by our old faith, have no desire for novelty, have nothing to add and nothing to take away from that which we have received from the Apostles. That assembly dispersed. But its effect has remained. All of us heard this year with great interest of that testimony of affectionate regard which our brethren in the United States of America sent to England by the hands of the Bishops of Lichfield and Ohio, and which in the name of the Mother Church of England I had the privilege of accepting in the Cathedral of the metropolis. Everyone who fears lest wars and rumours of wars should keep good men asunder, must rejoice that in the Church of which we are members there is a pledge of brotherly affection and regard even amongst those who are separated by many political considerations.

The object of the Lambeth Conference, as you see, was confined entirely to bringing together the scattered members of our own communion; but we should form a very inaccurate estimate of our position in Christendom if, wide as we know the Church of England to be, in the extent to which it is diffused throughout the world, we did not recognize that there are many other bodies in Christendom besides that to which we belong.

Hence I have always looked with great interest on the exertions of the Anglo-Continental Society, which endeavours to spread throughout Europe a knowledge of the works of our great divines. I do not pledge myself to agree in all respects with the principles laid down by that Society, but no one, I think, can doubt that it is the duty of the Church of England to take some distinct steps to make its doctrines clearly known throughout the continent of Europe,—among Roman Catholics, and among other bodies who are generally very ignorant of the principles of our Church: and I believe you will find that the publication by this Society of works approved in the Church of England has been attended with a very good result in conciliating to our Church the friendship of many who are separated from it, and also in bringing before many who otherwise could not have received them the great Gospel doctrines on which our Church is founded.

A few weeks ago there met at Cologne the representatives of that body which has attracted so much attention lately in Germany,—the Old Catholics; and I, for my part, rejoice that two Bishops and another dignitary of the Church of England were present upon that occasion. I do not say that we can look with unfeigned satisfaction on the doctrinal statements which have been brought forward as yet by that body, but we could not fail to regard this meeting with great interest. Looking back in our own Church to the time which immediately preceded the Reformation, I suppose there is not one of us who does not venerate the names of Sir Thomas More, Archbishop Warham, and his friend Erasmus; and if we find men now much in the same position in which Erasmus stood to the predominating Christianity of his day, it would be very strange if we did not feel a Christian interest in the struggle through which they are called to pass.

But all these matters on which I have now touched

refer to a union either amongst ourselves as members of the Episcopal Church of England and its daughters, or to hopes of a union which may in some time to come be effected between this Episcopal Church of England and other Episcopal Churches from which at present we are greatly separated.

We have rejoiced, as the communication between ourselves and the East has increased, to welcome from time to time distinguished ecclesiastics of the Eastern Churches. Not that we are insensible to the grave errors which still overspread their several communions; but we are glad if any opportunity occurs for making them better acquainted with the Church of which we are members, and for doing them what good we can in a kindly spirit of brotherly love.

But everyone knows that the Episcopal Churches, widely as they are spread throughout the world, do not comprise the whole of Christendom. Everyone knows that we of the Church of England, in the early times of our history, after the Reformation, were much more connected with the non-episcopal than with the Episcopal communions; and therefore I for one am glad that good Archbishop Sumner, in his day, called together another assembly at Lambeth, at which I was present, the object of which was to foster brotherly love between ourselves and the Protestants of the Continent. I think it was right that Lambeth should be now, as it was formerly, the centre to which the Protestant Churches looked for help. And as there were gathered together on that occasion many of our own countrymen from whom usually we are separated, and all of us heartily prayed to God for blessings upon the pure Gospel of

Christ, wherever it was preached and whosoever were its ministers, so I think we shall fail of our duty if we confine our regard to the Episcopal Churches, and are not anxious to give the hand of brotherhood to others also with whom we are intimately connected in the bonds of a common faith.

I consider that it was a great privilege which I enjoyed as Bishop of London when, in the year 1862, the metropolis was full of strangers from all parts of the world, and when I had the opportunity of opening many of our chapels, so far as the law of the land allowed, to pastors from Germany, from France, from Switzerland, from the Waldensian Valleys; and I believe they went home with a kindly feeling of brotherly love, not only to the English Church but to the English nation generally, which it would have been difficult to foster without this kindly welcome. In our many unconsecrated places of worship which the law allowed to be so opened for their use, these pastors had, under the invitation of the authorities of the English Church, an opportunity each of preaching to his own people, in his own tongue, "the unsearchable riches of Christ."

No doubt also it is a grave and important subject for us to consider, that, while men are holding out the right hand of fellowship to the Episcopal Churches of the Continent, there are so many of our own brethren at home from whom we are estranged. Every effort which can be made to unite us more truly in the bonds of Christian love with these our brethren at home, seems to come to us recommended by something more practical than is found in efforts to unite with foreigners, many of whom show little inclination to admit us to their fellowship, and some of whom could not admit us, without our denying the great principles of our Reformed Church. I am no visionary looking forward to a time when all the various denominations throughout Britain are to come and desire admission into the Church of England; but still I think, if we persevere in the loving, faithful discharge of our duty, if we adhere faithfully to the formularies which we have received from the time of the Reformation, and if we show in all things, where we can without any compromise of principle, a hearty spirit of Christian love, there is every hope that in Christ's good time the differences that keep us apart may disappear.

Now the peculiar qualification which the Church of England possesses for thus working for the union of divided Christendom, springs from the twofold character impressed on it by the mode in which its Reformation was conducted. There was no rash severance from the past, and therefore we retain all Catholic doctrine and many old Catholic forms, and present to those who have not yet passed through a Reformation many features which attract them, and without which we should have little hope of bringing them to a better mind. And with regard to the other features of our Church,—that steady adherence to the written Word of God, that distinct maintenance of the Reformation formularies which has hitherto characterized us,—these do give us great power of influencing other Protestant bodies from which we have been long estranged.

If you cast your eyes over the state of Europe at this moment, you will, I think, have a very uneasy feeling as to the present prospects of religion. You see infidelity in two forms, either in the shape of cold indifference or of that coarse and violent Atheism which has hurried men to such brutal acts in a neighbouring country. How far is its influence spread; and in most of the countries of the Continent, or at least of Southern Europe, how little is there to oppose it! You see superstition bursting forth occasionally, in the midst of the light of this nineteenth century, into acts of idolatry which we should scarcely have thought possible in the darkest age before the Reformation. Here then seems to be the only alternative which in most of these countries is presented to earnest-minded men—either float with the current of the age and give up Christianity altogether, or make a stern resistance to it in the spirit of the most narrow-minded bigotry and superstition. Can we then venture to stand apart from the efforts of those struggling communities which uphold Gospel truth in the midst of prevailing error? Switzerland and all Protestant Europe are now mourning the loss of Merle d'Aubigné; and in France the greatest of her living statesmen is contending in his old age for the maintenance of pure religion. The Church of England dare not show indifference to the cause so dear to these men's hearts. In Germany indeed we may hope that the state of matters is better; but still the view is nowhere satisfactory. In this our Church of England, I think we find the sole example of a Church at once holding all the old ceremonials, as far as they are consistent with the Scriptures and the teaching of the immediate successors of the Apostles, and at the same time showing a readiness to admit all the light which our growing intelligence in this age places within our reach.

It is commonly said now-a-days in many countries that Christianity and Reason must be divorced; that Christianity and Civilization,—modern Civilization,—are antagonists to each other. Certainly we, in the Church of England, have no fear lest there should be any real antagonism between God's two great lights to man,—Reason, and Science as its product, on the one hand, and Revelation on the other. We, of this free country, who desire to see civilization spread far and wide, and who recognize in civilization the perfection of humanity, have no fear lest the human race, as it approaches perfection, should more and more separate itself from Him who is the model of all perfection. We have no fears lest Science and Reason should be found irreconcilable with the truth of God. We have no fear lest the perfection of civil society should be found inconsistent with the perfection of that ecclesiastical society to which we belong.

There are certain names which occur to us, of famous ministers of the Church of England,—Richard Whately, Thomas Arnold, Julius Hare, Frederick Maurice, Frederick Robertson,—I name only those who have gone to their rest;—these are not the names of the clergy who are most popular throughout England, but I am bold to maintain that they are the names of men who have done a good work in their day and generation, for their very presence amongst us has been a standing protest against any notion that inquiry and the fearless love of truth can be inconsistent with the Gospel which we preach. These men,—had they lived under another system, and in another age, it might have been very difficult to say what would have become of them. They could not certainly have joined the Church of Rome without crushing their convictions, as many have done in past times, under the weight of an overwhelming tyranny, or seeking relief from their doubts and scruples by a silence akin to death. But also I say, these men could not well have found a home in any of the ordinary sects which exist amongst us. It is then, I am bold to say, no blame to the Church of England, but rather it may be its pride, that it is able to include amongst its ministers the most active and inquiring intellects, and that it has no fear lest a bold examination of truth should destroy those truths of God on which it teaches men to depend for their salvation.

Such then I believe to be the sort of position which the Church of England occupies at this time. On the right hand and on the left it invites to fellowship those from whom others are necessarily entirely separated; but let it not be supposed that on this account there is any faltering as to the maintenance of Christ's truth in the Church to which we belong, or that a mere system of indifferentism is put up in place of that Gospel which we prize. If men desire to corrupt the pure Gospel of Christ, either by unauthorized additions, or by watering it down so that it becomes a mere sentimentalism, the Church of England has no word of encouragement for either of these mistakes. I desire that all persons who are alienated from the Church of England at this time should read carefully its formularies and the books of its great writers, to whatever school they belong,—that it should be understood that the

Church of England protests now, as much as it ever did, against all errors which are anti-Christian or which corrupt Christianity; while in the wide spirit of comprehensive love it desires to draw into its fold all those who are faithful to the Lord Jesus Christ.

Does anyone say that there is faltering in our views as to the errors of the Church of Rome? Does the Church of Rome teach a doctrine respecting the blessed sacrament of the Eucharist which, beginning in superstition, generally ends in idolatry? Does not the Church of England, with unfaltering voice, declare against the Romish doctrine of transubstantiation? Does it not declare that the mean whereby we feed upon the body and blood of Christ is faith? Hence it is consistent in adopting the Rubric appended to the Communion of the Sick, which says that a faithful and penitent man, who is prevented by lack of opportunity from receiving the outward elements, doth yet eat and drink the Body and Blood of Christ to his soul's health, though the outward communion be altogether absent. For our Church has distinctly asserted in her Articles that Christ's Body when present in the Eucharist is there only after a heavenly and spiritual manner, and in the famous Rubric at the end of the Communion Service that no adoration "ought to be done either unto the Sacramental Bread and Wine there bodily received, or unto any corporal presence of Christ's natural Flesh and Blood. For the Sacramental Bread and Wine remain still in their very natural substances, and therefore may not be adored (for that were idolatry, to be abhorred of all faithful Christians): and the natural Body and Blood of our Saviour Christ are in Heaven, and not here; it being against the truth of Christ's natural Body to be at one time in more places than one." Does not all this set before us distinctly that the Church of England is faithful now, as it ever was, to that scriptural doctrine of the Eucharist, which our fathers died to maintain?

Again, does the Church of Rome tell us that the Bible is not sufficient; that there must be other teachers and another system of inspiration besides that which comes down to us from Christ and His Apostles in the written Word? Does not the Church of England tell us that neither any particular Church nor yet any gathered assembly of the universal Church is free from error, and that the only hope of the Church is to keep stedfast by the written Word?

Does the Church of Rome, with faltering voice, hesitate as to how we are accounted righteous before God; setting forth indeed the Lord Jesus Christ as our atonement, but telling us that partly by sacraments, and partly by works, and partly by faith, we become partakers of justification? The Church of England has no hesitation in saying, as it said of old, that the doctrine that we are justified by faith only is a most wholesome doctrine. And whatever other errors there may be of the Church of Rome which militate against the pure Apostolic faith, to all of them we may find an antidote in the approved formularies of our Church and the writings of our divines.

Or, on the other hand, would anyone say that our Christianity may become a sort of half infidelity? Who can read the formularies of the Church of England without seeing that the person of Christ, His incarnation, His death for our sins, His intercession for us at the Father's right hand, His gift of the Holy Spirit, is set before us in every page? Who can doubt that the Church of England upholds the doctrine of the personality of the Holy Ghost, and teaches us, depending alone on the merits of our Lord and Saviour Jesus Christ, to pray for the influence of the personal Comforter that we may be brought to our risen Lord?

My friends, I do believe that with the clearest and most unhesitating maintenance of the great Gospel truths, with the clearest protest against errors which are dangerous to the soul, on one side and on the other, the Church of England still stretches wide its arms and desires to bring souls to God, and is antagonistic to no Church or individual, so far as that Church or individual is faithful to the Lord Jesus Christ.

And now, my friends, if this be the work of the Church of England, how shall he answer for it who thwarts its fulfilment of its sacred mission? How shall he answer for it if, by violent assaults from without or faithlessness from within, he injures this great cause? How shall any of us answer for it if, through a restless disobedience to authority, a straining after novelties unheard of before, or the revival of old exploded errors, we injure this great Church of Christ,—how shall we answer for it if we fail through any cold indifference to the great doctrines which our Church upholds? Still more, how shall we answer for it if, through listless neglect of duty, thoughtlessness as to the value of the souls the Lord has committed to us, we do the Church far greater injury even than could be inflicted on it by false doctrine—the injury which flows from a false and sinful life?

Our years, my friends, are passing with marvellous rapidity. Our homes, our Church, the nation, all testify, through the changes which are passing over them, that the time of our trial is short. God grant that, when it is over, you and I and all of us may be found to have been faithful in our day and generation to the great work entrusted to us by the Lord.

APPENDICES.

APPENDICES.

A.

CANTERBURY DIOCESAN EDUCATION SOCIETY.

Secretaries. { Rev. E. Gilder, St. Dunstan's, Canterbury.
{ Rev. T. G. Carter, Linton, Maidstone.

The Society, established in 1839, after having been actively engaged ever since in promoting the establishment and efficiency of Church schools in the diocese, has during the last four years accomplished the following results, including its special efforts to meet recent legislation:—

FUNDS.

In answer to a special appeal made by the Archbishop in 1870 for funds to assist parishes in the diocese in meeting the demands for additional accommodation, and to maintain a second diocesan inspector, there have been contributed—

Special Subscriptions and Donations	£3,582 3 0
Collections made, in conformity with a Pastoral Letter, in 145 Churches	743 10 7
Total ordinary Subscriptions for four years	2,133 18 4
Total Receipts	£6,459 11 11

BUILDING GRANTS.

During the same period of four years the following Grants have been made:—

For Building, Enlarging, and Fitting-up Schools and Teachers' Houses:—

Grants amounting to	£4,360.
In	114 Parishes.
Affording additional accommodation for	8,847 Scholars.
And additional residences for	27 Teachers.
At an estimated cost of	£59,640 19s. 9d.

A few of these undertakings have not been completed. As a matter of fact, however, those that are completed will be found to have cost much more than was expected, so that the whole sum expended will be quite as great as has been stated above.

DIOCESAN MONITORS.

During the same period seventy-nine diocesan monitors have been appointed and paid by the Society, in as many schools, for periods of service not exceeding five years. These monitors have been annually examined by the diocesan inspector, and many of them have become pupil-teachers. The amount of grants paid for this object has been 369*l*.

EVENING SCHOOLS.

Grants have been made to 155 evening schools amounting to 353*l*. 13*s*. 6*d*., at a rate varying from three shillings to half-a-crown on behalf of each scholar whose proper attendance and conduct was duly certified, on condition that some religious instruction was given.

DIOCESAN INSPECTION.

The Society made itself liable in November 1870 for the salary of a second diocesan inspector; and an offer of inspection in religious knowledge is now made annually to every Church school in the diocese, and has been almost universally accepted. This involves an annual charge on the Society of 450*l*., towards which the Society for Promoting Christian Knowledge contributed for the first year 100*l*.

The work of the diocesan inspectors for the first completed year has been as follows:—

	Schools inspected.	Scholars on Books.	Scholars examined.
Rev. B. F. Smith	223	22,967	16,280
Rev. E. W. Knollys	217	22,388	16,492
Total	440	45,355	32,772

The diocesan inspectors also examined in religious knowledge 246 pupil teachers at collective examinations and 21 in private.

PRAYER-BOOK PRIZE SCHEME.

A scheme for examining elder children in parochial schools in the knowledge of the Prayer-book was set on foot by the Society in 1871. Small grants were voted to each local board willing to expend an equal sum in prizes for successful candidates. The first examination was held in March 1872, in which 100 candidates satisfied the examiners and were classified in three classes.

B.

CANTERBURY DIOCESAN CHURCH BUILDING AND ENDOWMENT SOCIETY.

ESTABLISHED JANUARY 27TH, 1865.

Hon. Sec.—REV. W. FIELD, GODMERSHAM VICARAGE.

OBJECTS OF THE SOCIETY.

1. The erection of churches and chapels, the purchase of buildings to be used as churches or chapels, and the enlargement, increase, or improvement of the accommodation of existing churches and chapels.

2. The endowment of buildings intended to be consecrated as churches and chapels, by augmenting local benefactions raised for that purpose. The grants in such cases not to be paid until the buildings shall have been consecrated.

3. The increase of such endowments of existing churches and chapels as do not afford a stipend of 200*l.* a year to the incumbents; by augmenting local benefactions raised for that purpose.

4. The increase, by annual grants, of incomes of incumbents who do not receive a net stipend of 150*l.* a year, in cases where there is a reasonable prospect of a permanent increase of such incomes, from the Ecclesiastical Commissioners or any other source.

5. The erection or enlargement of parsonage-houses, and the purchase or improvement of buildings to be used as parsonage-houses.

6. To promote the increase of church accommodation generally, by paying one-fourth of any sums collected in churches, in behalf of this Society, to the Incorporated Society for Building and Enlarging Churches and Chapels in England and Wales.

SUMMARY OF THE SOCIETY'S OPERATIONS FROM ITS COMMENCEMENT.

	Number of Churches assisted.	Additional Seats.	Amount of Society's Grants. £	Total Cost. £
New Churches	15	6,714	4,470	46,683
Churches rebuilt	4	728	416	9,032
Churches enlarged or improved	52	6,623	5,152	58,393
Temporary Churches	6	1,511	377	3,271
	77	15,576	10,415	117,379
Increase of Small Benefices	19		2,975	...
Parsonage-houses	35		5,550	52,140
Annual Grants to Incorporated Church Building Society	...	...	1,185	...
	131	15,576	£20,125	£169,519

The Archbishop strongly urges on his Clergy to have parochial collections for this and the Educational Society.

C.

STATUTES OF CANTERBURY CATHEDRAL.

The Statutes of Canterbury Cathedral, drawn up by Archbishop Laud, and confirmed by King Charles I., A.D. 1636, are given in Laud's Works (Library of Anglo-Catholic Theology), vol. v. part ii. pp. 506—545. They are accompanied by a letter from the King, and there is also a letter from the Archbishop given in vol. vi., part ii., p. 484.

"I left out divers superstitions which were in the old book, and ordained many sermons in their room," writes the Archbishop in his "Troubles and Trials" (iv. 224).

D.

THE ACT OF UNIFORMITY AMENDMENT ACT.

The Act of Uniformity Amendment Act, 1872 (35 & 36 Vict. ch. 35), contains the following provisions:—

1. The Shortened Order for Morning Prayer or for Evening Prayer, specified in the Schedule to this Act, may, on any day except Sunday, Christmas Day, Ash Wednesday, Good Friday, and Ascension Day, be used, if in a cathedral in addition to, and if in a church in lieu of, the Order for Morning Prayer or for Evening Prayer respectively prescribed by the Book of Common Prayer.

2. Upon any special occasion approved by the Ordinary, there may be used in any cathedral or church a special form of service approved by the Ordinary, so that there be not introduced into such service anything, except anthems or hymns, which does not form part of the Holy Scriptures or Book of Common Prayer.

3. An additional form of service varying from any form prescribed by the Book of Common Prayer may be used at any

hour on any Sunday or holy-day in any cathedral or church in which there are duly read, said, or sung as required by law on such Sunday or holy-day at some other hour or hours the Order for Morning Prayer, the Litany, such part of the Order for the Administration of the Lord's Supper or Holy Communion as is required to be read on Sundays and holy-days if there be no Communion, and the Order for Evening Prayer; so that there be not introduced into such additional service any portion of the Order for the Administration of the Lord's Supper or Holy Communion, or anything, except anthems or hymns, which does not form part of the Holy Scriptures or Book of Common Prayer, and so that such form of service and the mode in which it is used is for the time being approved by the Ordinary: provided that nothing in this section shall affect the use of any portion of the Book of Common Prayer as otherwise authorized by the Act of Uniformity or this Act.

4. Whereas doubts have arisen as to whether the following forms of service, that is to say, the Order for Morning Prayer, the Litany, and the Order for the Administration of the Lord's Supper or Holy Communion, may be used as separate services, and it is expedient to remove such doubts: Be it therefore enacted and declared, that any of such forms of service may be used together or in varying order as separate services, or that the Litany may be said after the third collect in the Order for Evening Prayer, either in lieu of or in addition to the use of the Litany in the Order for Morning Prayer, without prejudice nevertheless to any legal powers vested in the Ordinary; and any of the said forms of service may be used with or without the preaching of a sermon or lecture, or the reading of a homily.

5. Whereas doubts have arisen as to whether a sermon or lecture may be preached without the common prayers and services appointed by the Book of Common Prayer for the time of day being previously read, and it is expedient to remove such doubts: Be it therefore enacted and declared, that a sermon or lecture may be preached without the common prayers or services appointed by the Book of Common Prayer being read before it is preached, so that such sermon or lecture be preceded by any service authorized by this Act, or by the Bidding Prayer, or by

a collect taken from the Book of Common Prayer, with or without the Lord's Prayer.

SCHEDULE.

Note.—The Minister using the Shortened Order for Morning Prayer or for Evening Prayer in this Schedule, may in his discretion add in its proper place any exhortation, prayer, canticle, hymn, psalm, or lesson contained in the Order for Morning Prayer or for Evening Prayer in the Book of Common Prayer and omitted or authorized to be omitted from such Shortened Order.

Each of the twenty-two portions into which the one hundred and nineteenth psalm is divided in the Book of Common Prayer shall be deemed, for the purposes of this Schedule, to be a separate psalm.

SHORTENED FORMS OF SERVICE.

THE SHORTENED ORDER FOR MORNING PRAYER DAILY THROUGHOUT THE YEAR, EXCEPT ON SUNDAY, CHRISTMAS DAY, ASH WEDNESDAY, GOOD FRIDAY, AND ASCENSION DAY.

At the beginning of Morning Prayer the Minister shall read with a loud voice some one or more of these sentences of the Scriptures that follow.

When the wicked man, &c.

A General Confession to be said of the whole Congregation after the Minister, all kneeling.

Almighty and most merciful Father, &c.

The Absolution, or Remission of sins, to be pronounced by the Priest alone, standing; the people still kneeling.

Almighty God, the Father, &c.

The people shall answer here, and at the end of all other prayers, Amen.

Then the Minister shall kneel, and say the Lord's Prayer with an audible voice; the people also kneeling, and repeating it with him.

Our Father, which art in heaven, &c.

Then likewise he shall say,

O Lord, open thou our lips.
&c. &c. &c.

Here, all standing up, the Priest shall say,

Glory be to the Father, &c.

Then shall follow one or more of the Psalms appointed. And at the end of every Psalm throughout the year, and likewise at the end of Benedicite, Benedictus, Magnificat, *and* Nunc dimittis, *shall be repeated,*

Glory be to the Father, &c.

Then shall be read distinctly, with an audible voice, either the First Lesson taken out of the Old Testament as is appointed in the Calendar, or the Second Lesson taken out of the New Testament, except there be a Proper Lesson assigned for that day, in which case the Proper Lesson shall be read, and if there are two Proper Lessons each shall be read in its proper place; he that readeth so standing and turning himself as he may best be heard of all such as are present.

Note that before every Lesson the Minister shall say, Here beginneth such a Chapter, *or* Verse of such a Chapter, of such a Book. *And after every Lesson,* Here endeth the Lesson, *or* the First *or* the Second Lesson.

And after the Lesson, or between the First and Second Lessons, shall be said or sung in English one of the following:—

Either the Hymn called Te Deum Laudamus.

We praise thee, O God, &c.

Or this Canticle, Benedicite, omnia opera.

O all ye works of the Lord, &c.

Or the Hymn following (except when that shall happen to be read in the Lesson for the day, or for the Gospel on Saint John Baptist's Day):

Benedictus. St. Luke i. 68.

Blessed be the Lord God of Israel, &c.

APPENDICES.

Or this Psalm:

Jubilate Deo.

O be joyful in the Lord, all ye lands, &c.

Then shall be sung or said the Apostles' Creed by the Minister and the people standing.

I believe in God the Father Almighty, &c.

And after that, the people all devoutly kneeling, the Minister shall pronounce with a loud voice,

The Lord be with you.
Answer. And with thy spirit.
Minister. Let us pray.

Then the Priest shall say,

O Lord, shew thy mercy upon us.
&c. &c. &c.

Then shall follow three Collects. The first of the day, which shall be the same that is appointed at the Communion; the second for Peace; the third for grace to live well; and the two last Collects shall never alter, but daily be said at Morning Prayer throughout all the year, as followeth, all kneeling.

The second Collect for Peace.

O God, who art the Author of peace, &c.

The third Collect for Grace.

O Lord, our heavenly Father, &c.

Here may follow an Anthem or Hymn:
Then these two Prayers following:

A Prayer of Saint Chrysostome.

Almighty God, who hast given us grace, &c.

2 Corinthians xiii.

The grace of our Lord Jesus Christ, &c.

Here endeth the Shortened Order of Morning Prayer.

APPENDICES.

THE SHORTENED ORDER FOR EVENING PRAYER DAILY THROUGHOUT THE YEAR, EXCEPT ON SUNDAY, CHRISTMAS DAY, ASH WEDNESDAY, GOOD FRIDAY, AND ASCENSION DAY.

At the beginning of Evening Prayer the Minister shall read with a loud voice some one or more of these sentences of the Scriptures that follow :—

When the wicked man, &c.

A general Confession to be said of the whole Congregation after the Minister, all kneeling.

Almighty and most merciful Father, &c.

The Absolution, or Remission of sins, to be pronounced by the Priest alone, standing; the people still kneeling.

Almighty God, the Father, &c.

Then the Minister shall kneel, and say the Lord's Prayer; the people also kneeling, and repeating it with him.

Our Father, which art in heaven, &c.

Then likewise he shall say,

O Lord, open thou our lips.

Here all standing up, the Priest shall say,

Glory be to the Father, &c.

Then shall be said or sung one or more of the Psalms in order as they be appointed. Then either a Lesson of the Old Testament as is appointed, or a Lesson of the New Testament as it is appointed, except there be a Proper Lesson assigned for that day, in which case the Proper Lesson shall be read, and if there are two Proper Lessons each shall be read in its proper place; and after the Lesson, or between the First and Second Lessons, shall be said or sung in English one of the following :—

Either Magnificat, *or the Song of the Blessed* Virgin Mary, *in English, as follows :—*

Magnificat. St. Luke i.

My soul doth magnify the Lord, &c.

Or this Psalm (except it be on the nineteenth day of the month, when it is read in the ordinary course of the Psalms):

Cantate Domino. Psalm xcviii.
O sing unto the Lord a new song, &c.

Or Nunc dimittis (*or the Song of* Simeon), *as followeth:*
Nunc dimittis. St. Luke ii. 29.
Lord, now lettest thou thy servant, &c.

Or else this Psalm (except it be on the twelfth day of the month):
Deus misereatur. Psalm lxvii.
God be merciful unto us, and bless us, &c.

Then shall be said or sung the Apostles' Creed by the Minister and the people, standing:
I believe in God the Father Almighty, &c.

And after that, the people all devoutly kneeling, the Minister shall pronounce with a loud voice,
The Lord be with you.
Answer. And with thy spirit.
Minister. Let us pray.

Then the Priest shall say,
O Lord, shew thy mercy upon us.
&c. &c. &c.

Then shall follow three Collects. The first of the day; the second for Peace; the third for aid against all perils, as hereafter followeth; which two last Collects shall be daily said at Evening prayer without Alteration.
The second Collect at Evening Prayer.
O God, from whom all holy desires, &c.

The third Collect for Aid against all Perils.
Lighten our darkness, &c.

Here may follow an Anthem or Hymn.

A Prayer of Saint Chrysostome.
Almighty God, who hast given us grace, &c.

2 Corinthians xiii.
The grace of our Lord Jesus Christ, &c.

Here endeth the Shortened Order of Evening Prayer.

E.

THE SOCIETY FOR THE RELIEF OF THE WIDOWS AND ORPHANS OF THE DIOCESE.

A good account of the Society will be found in the Canterbury Diocesan Calendar, p. 41. This carefully-edited and valuable publication contains a large amount of information on all matters connected with the Diocese, as well as concerning the Church generally.

F.

ASSOCIATION OF LAY HELPERS.

The Association of Lay Helpers for the Diocese of London, for gratuitous assistance to the Clergy in their parochial work, was formed in May 1865, on a Report presented by the Sub-Committee of the Bishop of London's Fund on Lay Agency. The number of members of this Association has steadily increased each year, and has now reached over 1,400, in which number of course are included many persons who were working in their several parishes before the Association was formed. But the progress of the Association may be seen by the following statement of the number of members each year:—

		Lay Helpers.	Lay Readers.
Midsummer,	1867	90	—
,,	1868	187	—
,,	1869	383	—
,,	1870	836	18
,,	1871	1,393	30

The following *Rules* and *Suggestions* are taken from the last London Report. Some of them are obviously suited more for a town than a country diocese:—

RULES.

1. Persons desiring to become Members of the Association (who must be Communicants) shall offer themselves or be proposed to the Bishop.

2. A register of the names and addresses of the Members shall be kept, showing what description of work each unemployed Member may be willing to undertake, and also the place and the nature of the work in which each employed Member is engaged.

3. Upon the application of Incumbents, Members of the Association shall be put into communication with them, with a view to such arrangements for lay assistance in parochial work as may be mutually agreed upon.

4. Once in every year the Members shall have the opportunity of attending Divine Service and receiving the Holy Communion together.

5. Once, at least, in every year, a Meeting of the Members shall be held, under the presidency of the Bishop if possible, in order to consult together upon one or more of the various branches of work in which they are engaged, and to make such regulations in regard to their own proceedings as may from time to time be found necessary or expedient.

6. The Executive Committee shall be appointed by the Bishop, year by year, at the Annual Meeting.

SUGGESTIONS AS TO THE KINDS OF WORK OPEN TO LAYMEN.

I. SUNDAY WORK.

1. Superintendence of, or teaching in, Sunday Schools, seeking out children who do not go to School, conducting Special Morning Services for young children, also Evening Services for children.

2. Conducting Bible Classes for young men, also Classes for children or others held at the Teacher's own house.

3. Systematically visiting the poor and sick for religious conversation and instruction, both at their own homes and at Hospitals and Workhouse Infirmaries.

4. Conducting or assisting at Services for the poor in School and Mission Rooms, and in the open air.

5. Attending and taking part at religious discussions among the working classes.

6. Distributing tracts in the streets and parks, and also from house to house.

7. Assisting at Church Services, as members of choirs, by reading the lessons, or attending to the comfortable seating of the poor.

8. Seeking out the unbaptized and unconfirmed, encouraging the newly confirmed to come to Holy Communion, inducing the poor to attend Church.

II. EVENING WORK.

1. Teaching in Night and Ragged Schools.

2. Management of Working Men's Clubs and Youth's Institutes; assistance at popular Lectures, Penny Readings, and other means of recreation.

3. Attendance at Penny Banks, Clothing Funds, and School and Parochial Libraries.

4. Visiting the poor, either generally or in a defined district, the families in which shall be considered especially as under the care of the visitor.

5. Assisting in and conducting Services in School and Mission Rooms and the open air.

6. Assisting in Church Services as above, also practising Church and School Choirs.

III. DAY WORK.

1. Visiting the poor and sick.

2. Superintending the distribution of relief.

3. Reading and speaking to working men on religious subjects in workshops.

4. Collecting and canvassing for funds for Parochial and Mission purposes.

5. Acting as Secretaries to Parochial Institutions and Religious and Charitable Societies.

IV. GENERAL WORK.

Endeavouring by personal influence and exertions to further the cause of Lay Agency, so as to strengthen the hands of those already labouring in the work, and encourage others to follow their example.

The following is the form used for admitting Lay Associates in the Diocese of Canterbury :—

𝕬𝖗𝖈𝖍𝖎𝖇𝖆𝖑𝖉 𝕮𝖆𝖒𝖕𝖇𝖊𝖑𝖑, by Divine Providence 𝕬𝖗𝖈𝖍𝖇𝖎𝖘𝖍𝖔𝖕 𝖔𝖋 𝕮𝖆𝖓𝖙𝖊𝖗𝖇𝖚𝖗𝖞, to our beloved and approved in Christ greeting: 𝖂𝖊 do, by these presents, give unto you our Commission to act as Reader in the Parish of   within our Diocese and jurisdiction, on the nomination of the Rev.   of the same, 𝕬𝖓𝖉 𝖉𝖔 authorize you, subject to his approval, to read Prayers and to read and explain the Holy Scriptures in the School thereof, or in other rooms within the said Parish, and generally to render aid to the Incumbent in all ministrations which do not strictly require the service of a Minister in Holy Orders; 𝕬𝖓𝖉 𝖜𝖊 further authorize you to render similar aid in other Parishes in our Diocese, at the written request, in each case, of the Incumbent; 𝕬𝖓𝖉 𝖜𝖊 hereby declare that this our Commission shall remain valid until it shall be revoked by us or our successors (whether *mero motu*, or at the written request of the said   ), or until a fresh admission to the said Parish of   shall have been made. And so we commend you to ALMIGHTY GOD, Whose blessing we humbly pray may rest upon you and your work.

𝕲𝖎𝖛𝖊𝖓 under our hand and seal this   day of   in the year of our LORD One thousand eight hundred and

G.

CONFIRMATIONS.

Number of Confirmations.		Number of Candidates.		Total.
		MALE.	FEMALE.	
1869	41	3,323	4,158	7,481
1870	34	1,811	2,607	4,418
1871	78	2,353	3,680	6,033
1872	78	2,505	3,035	5,540

The proportion of Males to Females in 1869 was about 80 to 100.
,, ,, ,, ,, 1870 ,, 69 ,,
,, ,, ,, ,, 1871 ,, 64 ,,
,, ,, ,, ,, 1872 ,, 82 ,,

H.

THE CHURCH PENITENTIARY ASSOCIATION AND THE STONE PENITENTIARY, DARTFORD.

From papers issued by the Church Penitentiary Association it appears that in twenty-nine towns in Kent, with an aggregate population of 420,252, there have been found 994 women who are fitting objects for a Penitentiary. No doubt this number falls far below the real total, even in the places where inquiries have been instituted.

The total number of Refuges and Lock-wards in Kent is six, containing accommodation for 160 persons.

The Stone Penitentiary is carried on upon the system of *self-devotion* to the work on the part of refined and educated

Ladies, serving for love's sake in the management of the poor inmates.

The Council now desires to raise 6,000*l.*; half of this to pay off the debt (which would free the Institution to the extent of 300*l.* a year—150*l.* instalment and 150*l.* interest), and half to complete the building, so as to admit from 80 to 100 inmates.

The annual subscriptions would be almost sufficient for the successful working of the Institution were it freed from the payment of this 300*l.*, and one nobleman in Kent (Lord Amherst) has offered to commence with a subscription of 100*l.*, if others will follow his example.

The local secretaries of the Council strongly desire—

(i.) A special agency in every town, under the Clergy.

(ii.) The formation in every town and populous parish of several district temporary refuges, near the worst part of the place, under the charge of a Mission-woman, or of some trustworthy woman of the labouring class.

(iii.) A larger number of *self-devoted ladies* who will either join existing institutions, or under wise and discreet supervision create new institutions.

It is the opinion of many persons that the supply of self-devoted women would be largely increased if episcopal visitation and supervision were secured in all cases.

The Archbishop of Canterbury and the Bishop of Rochester have given their full approval to the Stone Institution, and are much interested in the work.

At present there is a lamentable want of machinery throughout the diocese of Canterbury, to rescue the lost and to guide and strengthen them until they can return to their homes and earn their living honestly and respectably.

I.

ST. PETER'S ORPHAN AND CONVALESCENT HOME, ISLE OF THANET.

This Institution, begun in December 1869, is now finished, and at present contains forty-five orphans and a varying number of women and children requiring sea-air. The payment for orphans is 12*l.* a year, for convalescents 7*s.* per week.

Mrs. Tait will be thankful for any contributions to pay off the debt on the building and to fit and furnish it, as well as to provide a play-ground. For these purposes 3,800*l.* is required.

K.

THE CHURCH OF ENGLAND TEMPERANCE SOCIETY.

The Church of England Temperance Society was formed in 1862.

A Diocesan Society for the Dioceses of Chester and Manchester was established at a later period, and has attained to considerable dimensions and influence in the North of England.

The General and Diocesan Societies are now united, with the sanction of the two Archbishops, with committees and head offices at London and Manchester.

The objects of the Society are:—

1. The reformation of the intemperate.
2. The removal of the causes which lead to intemperance.

More particularly, it adopts as its basis of action the recommendations combined in the reports of the Committees on

Intemperance, presented to the Houses of Convocation of Canterbury and York.

The head offices are:—London: 6, Adam St., Adelphi; Manchester: 14, City Buildings; where the Report of the Society may be procured.

The Committee of Convocation referred to in the Charge have laid down the following principles:—

1. That the Church of Christ is the great Temperance Society of the world; and that if all Christians were careful to fulfil the vows and promises of their baptism, the evils of intemperance would soon disappear.

2. That it is the duty of all members of the Church, whether Clergy or Laity, to use their utmost efforts, both by precept and by example, to counteract this great social evil.

3. That there are cases of inveterate habits of intemperance in which no remedy short of "total abstinence" can avail for cure.

4. That there are many devout and conscientious persons, free from any temptations to this vice, who feel that from various causes, whether for the sake of their own health or for the sake of the example to others, they are bound to "total abstinence." But that these are "cases of conscience," by which the liberty of others is not to be judged or fettered.

L.

SPECIAL SERVICES FOR 20th DECEMBER.

The following Service is authorized for the Diocese of Canterbury, to be used on the 20th of December next, the Day of Intercession for an increased Supply of Missionaries.

The SERVICE may take one of two forms:—*Either* Special Psalms and Lessons with the Proper Sentences and any of the selected Collects may be incorporated, at the discretion of the Minister, in the ordinary Service for the day; *or* the whole, or any portion of the Service, as printed below, may be used as an additional Service after the Litany, or after the third Collect in Morning or Evening Prayer.

Where the HOLY COMMUNION is administered, one or more of the above Collects may be used, and the following Epistle and Gospel substituted for the ordinary Epistle and Gospel:—

For the Epistle, *Isaiah XLII.* 1—17.
For the Gospel, *St. Luke X.* 1—18.

SPECIAL SERVICE ON THE DAY OF INTERCESSION FOR AN INCREASED SUPPLY OF MISSIONARIES.

(DECEMBER 20, 1872.)

Suggested for use under the Act 35 and 36 Vict. c. xxxv. in Churches where it is thought desirable to unite the Special Service of the day with the ordinary Morning and Evening Prayer.

SENTENCES, PSALMS, AND LESSONS, WHICH MAY BE USED AT MORNING OR EVENING PRAYER.

SENTENCES.

God will have all men to be saved, and to come unto the knowledge of the truth. 1 *Tim. II.* 4.

Not by might, nor by power, but by my Spirit, saith the Lord of Hosts. *Zech. IV.* 6.

My Spirit remaineth among you: fear ye not. *Hag. II.* 5.

Thou shalt go to all that I shall send thee, and whatsoever I command thee thou shalt speak. *Jer. I.* 7.

All the ends of the world shall remember themselves, and be turned to the Lord; and all the kindreds of the nations shall worship before him.

For the kingdom is the Lord's: and he is the governor among the people. *Psalm XXII.* 27, 28.

PSALMS.

One or more of the following :—

II.	*XLVII.*	*LXXII.*
XLV.	*LXVII.*	*XCVII.*
XLVI.	*LXVIII.*	

LESSONS.

The First Lesson for the day at Morning or Evening Prayer, or one of the following :—

Isaiah LII. 13, to end of *LIII.*	*Isaiah LX.*	*Ezekiel XXXIV.* 6—17.
Isaiah VI. 1—9.	*Isaiah LXI.*	*Daniel X.* 2—13.
Isaiah XLIX.	*Isaiah LXII.*	*Malachi I.* 7—12.

The Second Lesson for the Day at Morning or Evening Prayer, or one of the following :—

| *St. Matthew IX.* 35, to *X.* 2. | *St. Matt. XXVIII.* 16, to end. | *Ephes. III.* 1—13. |
| *St. Matthew XI.* 2. | | *Rev. V.* |

One of the following Canticles may be used after the Second Lesson :—Psalm XCVI. or *CX.*

APPENDICES.

INTERCESSIONS, *which may be used either after the Litany or after the Third Collect at Morning or Evening Prayer.*

The Minister standing shall say, The harvest truly is great, but the labourers are few: pray ye therefore the Lord of the harvest that he would send forth labourers into his harvest.

People. O Lord, hear our prayer, and let our cry come unto Thee.

Then shall they all kneel upon their knees, and the Priests and Clerks kneeling shall say this Psalm:

Have mercy upon me, O God, after thy great goodness: according to the multitude of thy mercies do away mine offences.

Wash me throughly from my wickedness: and cleanse me from my sins.

For I acknowledge my faults: and my sin is ever before me.

Against thee only have I sinned, and done this evil in thy sight: that thou mightest be justified in thy saying, and clear when thou art judged.

Behold, I was shapen in wickedness: and in sin hath my mother conceived me.

But lo, thou requirest truth in the inward parts: and shalt make me to understand wisdom secretly.

Thou shalt purge me with hyssop, and I shall be clean: thou shalt wash me, and I shall be whiter than snow.

Thou shalt make me hear of joy and gladness: that the bones which thou hast broken may rejoice.

Turn thy face away from my sins: and put out all my misdeeds.

Make me a clean heart, O God: and renew a right spirit within me.

Cast me not away from thy presence: and take not thy Holy Spirit from me.

O give me the comfort of thy help again: and stablish me with thy free Spirit.

Then shall I teach thy ways unto the wicked: and sinners shall be converted unto thee.

Deliver me from blood-guiltiness, O God, thou that art the

God of my health: and my tongue shall sing of thy righteousness.

Thou shalt open my lips, O Lord: and my mouth shall shew thy praise.

For thou desirest no sacrifice, else would I give it thee: but thou delightest not in burnt-offerings.

The sacrifice of God is a troubled spirit: a broken and contrite heart, O God, shalt thou not despise.

O be favourable and gracious unto Sion: build thou the walls of Jerusalem.

Then shalt thou be pleased with the sacrifice of righteousness, with the burnt-offerings and oblations: then shall they offer young bullocks upon thine altar.

Glory be to the Father, and to the Son : and to the Holy Ghost ;

As it was in the beginning, is now, and ever shall be : world without end. *Amen.*

Then shall be said the following Versicles and Responses by the Minister and People:

O Lord, revive Thy work.
In the midst of the years.

Arise, O God, and judge Thou the Earth.
For Thou shalt take all heathen to Thine inheritance.

Deliver us from blood-guiltiness, O God.
For we have left undone those things which we ought to have done.

Deliver us from all our offences.
And make us not a rebuke unto the foolish.

Shew Thy servants Thy work, and their children Thy glory.
Prosper Thou the work of our hands upon us, O prosper Thou our handy-work.

Awake, awake, put on strength, O Arm of the Lord.
Awake, as in the ancient days, in the generations of old.

Stir up Thy strength, and come and help us.
That Thy way may be known upon earth, Thy saving health among all nations.

Look upon the Covenant, O Lord.
For all the earth is full of darkness and cruel habitations.

Shew Thy marvellous loving-kindness, O Lord.
O send out Thy Light and Thy Truth.

When Thou lettest Thy Breath go forth they shall be made.
And Thou shalt renew the face of the earth.

Thou shalt shew us wonderful things in Thy righteousness, O God of our salvation.
Thou that art the hope of all the ends of the earth, and of them that remain in the broad sea.

All nations whom Thou hast made shall come and worship Thee, O Lord.
And shall glorify Thy Name.

And all men that see it shall say, This hath God done.
For they shall perceive that it is His work.

Be Thou exalted, Lord, in Thine own strength.
So will we sing and praise Thy power.

Let us pray.

Minister. O God, the Creator and Preserver of all mankind, we humbly beseech Thee for all sorts and conditions of men; that Thou wouldest be pleased to make Thy ways known unto them, Thy saving health unto all nations; through Jesus Christ our Lord. *Amen.*

O Merciful God, who hast made all men, and hatest nothing that Thou hast made, nor wouldest the death of a sinner, but rather that he should be converted and live; Have mercy upon all Jews, Turks, Infidels, and Heretics, and take from them all ignorance, hardness of heart, and contempt of Thy Word; and so fetch them home, blessed Lord, to Thy flock, that they may be saved among the remnant of the true Israelites, and be made one fold under one Shepherd, Jesus Christ our Lord, who liveth and reigneth with Thee and the Holy Spirit, one God, world without end. *Amen.*

Stir up, we beseech Thee, O Lord, the wills of Thy faithful people; that they, plenteously bringing forth the fruit of good works, may of Thee be plenteously rewarded; through Jesus Christ our Lord. *Amen.*

Almighty God, who didst give such grace unto Thy holy Apostle Saint Andrew, that he readily obeyed the calling of Thy Son Jesus Christ, and followed Him without delay; Grant unto us all, that we, being called by Thy Holy Word, may forthwith give up ourselves obediently to fulfil Thy holy commandments; through the same Jesus Christ our Lord. *Amen.*

O Almighty God, who by Thy Son Jesus Christ didst give to Thy Apostle Saint Peter many excellent gifts, and commandedst him earnestly to feed Thy flock; Make, we beseech Thee, all Bishops and Pastors diligently to preach Thy Holy Word, and the people obediently to follow the same, that they may receive the crown of everlasting glory; through Jesus Christ our Lord. *Amen.*

O Almighty and Everlasting God, who didst give to Thine Apostle Bartholomew grace truly to believe and to preach Thy Word; Grant, we beseech Thee, unto Thy Church, to love that Word which he believed, and both to preach and receive the same; through Jesus Christ our Lord. *Amen.*

O God, who, through the preaching of the blessed Apostle Saint Paul, hast caused the light of the Gospel to shine throughout the world; Grant, we beseech Thee, that we, having his wonderful conversion in remembrance, may shew forth our thankfulness unto Thee for the same, by following the holy doctrine which he taught; through Jesus Christ our Lord. *Amen.*

Almighty God, who shewest to them that be in error the light of Thy truth, to the intent that they may return into the way of righteousness; Grant unto all them that are admitted into the fellowship of Christ's Religion, that they may eschew those things that are contrary to their profession, and follow all such things as are agreeable to the same; through our Lord Jesus Christ. *Amen.*

Almighty God, who hast promised to hear the petitions of them that ask in Thy Son's Name; We beseech Thee mercifully to incline Thine ears to us that have made now our prayers and supplications unto Thee; and grant, that those things, which we have faithfully asked according to Thy will, may effectually be obtained to the relief of our necessity, and to the setting forth of Thy glory; through Jesus Christ our Lord. *Amen.*

Minister. The Lord bless thee, and keep thee: the Lord make his face shine upon thee, and be gracious unto thee. The Lord lift up his countenance upon thee, and give thee peace. *Numbers VI.* 24—26.

THE END.

LONDON : R. CLAY, SONS, AND TAYLOR, PRINTERS.

TAIT, A.C.
   The present condition of the
Church of England.

BX
.5099
.T3

www.ingramcontent.com/pod-product-compliance
Lightning Source LLC
Chambersburg PA
CBHW020105170426
43199CB00009B/402